The Heirloom Quilt

by *Yolande Filson* &
Roberta Przybylski

That Patchwork Place®

Dedication

To Maman and all the mothers who devoted their time teaching their daughters the art of sewing. Thank you for your enduring persistence and the special gift you bestowed upon us.

Credits

Editor-in-Chief	Barbara Weiland
Managing Editor	Greg Sharp
Copy Editor	Liz McGehee
Proofreader	Tina Cook
Design Director	Judy Petry
Text Design	Connie Lunde
Photography	Brent Kane
Photo Stylist	Susan I. Jones
Illustration and Graphics	André Samson

Mission Statement

We are dedicated to providing quality products that encourage creativity and promote self-esteem in our customers and our employees. We strive to make a difference in the lives we touch.

That Patchwork Place is an employee-owned, financially secure company.

The Heirloom Quilt©
©1994 by Yolande Filson and
Roberta Przybylski
That Patchwork Place, Inc.,
PO Box 118, Bothell, WA 98041-0118 USA
Printed in the United States of America
99 98 97 96 95 94   6 5 4 3 2 1

Filson, Yolande,
    The heirloom quilt / Yolande Filson and Roberta Przybylski.
        p. cm.
    Includes bibliographical references.
    ISBN 1-56477-072-9 :
    1. Patchwork—Patterns. 2. Quilting—Patterns. I. Przybylski,
Roberta, 1946-   . II. Title.
TT835.F54 1994
746.46—dc20   94-18420
                                                      CIP

Acknowledgments

This book is a triumph in perseverance and a tribute to the faith we had in ourselves that we could do it!

Over the course of a year, as we continually worked to improve the sewing directions and completed each stage involved in putting this work into print, we sometimes labeled it "Pandora's Box." When we assured ourselves that there just can't be much more to do, we encountered avalanches of must do, must include, must redo, etc., etc., etc. At times, we were overwhelmed by the work load but found great comfort in the fact that we could rely on each other to share the tasks.

Family members, friends, and so many people helped make this book a reality. We are indebted to them for their individual contributions and would like to thank:

Deanna Williams of Capitol Imports for all laces, embroideries, and batistes, courtesy of Capitol Imports, Tallahassee, Florida;

Jolene Checchin, fabric artist, for her dainty and exquisite painting on the pearl buttons for the Tic-tac-toe Board Game;

Karen Janis, owner and designer of Keepsake Treasures, for her tireless sewing of sample blocks and projects, especially the pink boudoir box;

Diane Goeke, one of our creative and avid supporters, for help in our original attempts at photography;

Linda Zachman, the first female president of ISMDA and owner of Linda Z's Sewing Center, for her support and the freedom she gave us to create unusual classes;

All students of Linda Z's Sewing Center Heirloom Club in 1991, Arlington Heights, Illinois: Theresa, Amy, Carol, Maryann, Pat, Leslie, Maureen, Diane, Kathy, Maria, Mary, Nina, Debbie, Peggy, Deanna, and Barb for attending class, finishing their blocks, sewing and giving honest evaluations, and expressing enthusiasm and encouragement. Special thanks to Chris, Mary, and Barb for completing the first three quilts in record time and acting as role models for the rest of the class;

Julianne Jackson for introducing Roberta to the feared computer and Alan Briggs for being there to successfully rescue her at all hours;

All the fabric stores in the greater Chicago area, especially:

Finn's Fabrics by Dyllis, Barrington, Illinois, where we met and nurtured our love of fine fabrics;

Linda Z's Sewing Center, Arlington Heights, Illinois, where we taught and found a home and students who love heirloom sewing as much as we do;

Sew Much Better, Palatine, Illinois, where they were willing to order buttons and charms for us in a timely fashion to meet our deadlines;

Tom of Portraits by Thomas, Barrington, Illinois, for his artistic eye in the authors' photos.

Chantal Filson, Yolande's daughter, a very gifted and intuitive writer, for her contribution of our opening poem, "Cycles";

And a special thank you to our respective families for listening to all our lace and batiste stories over and over again. For all your support, encouragement, and the corporate experiences you shared with us, and, of course, the missed meals without complaining, thank you, Dan and Ted.

CONTENTS

~ INTRODUCTION ~

It is difficult to define the exact moment when the idea for this book was born. People, places, events, and nostalgia all contributed to my first heirloom quilt book.

Heirloom sewing and quilting both have roots in the past and have always appealed to me on both a personal and professional level. I was raised in a French Victorian household in a small town in French-speaking Quebec. My mother, Maman, was an excellent seamstress, who used the finest batiste and laces. Therefore, as I grew up, I was surrounded by fabrics, trims, and laces. I assumed this was natural in every Canadian household.

Hospitality went hand in hand with my mother's love of sewing. Tea was served every day at 4:00 p.m. for anyone who came to call. Sewing tips, as well as gossip, were exchanged freely with friends.

When I had successfully accomplished certain sewing skills that my mother deemed essential for all young ladies at that time, such as buttons at age 5 and pattern drafting for my dolls at age 9, Maman promoted me to the sewing machine. It was love at first sight. The French nuns continued my sewing education. In class, I was not the best student in following directions, and my teachers felt compelled to garner stricter guidelines to curb my creativity. Eventually, I was able to put my technical and creative sewing-machine skills to good use because of my petite size and scarcity of available clothing. It was there in my sewing room that I realized my love for fabrics, color, and creativity. I haven't stopped sewing since!

Necessity required that I study fashion design. I find it quite ironic that although I made many elaborate couture garments over the years, I was wearing an airline uniform when I met the man of my dreams! Go figure!

My life changed after having two children and moving thirteen times all over the United States and the world with my family. In between moves, I designed a line of girls' clothing, opened a fabric store, and attended numerous heirloom sewing and quilting seminars. Then the time came for me to share my sewing knowledge and experiences. I combined my two favorite topics, heirloom sewing and quilting, and began an heirloom club at a local fabric store that specialized in heirloom laces as well as smocking supplies. A "block a month" in heirloom laces with a quilt as the finished project was my goal. The response was better than I had hoped. The first month, thirty-five people told me an idea was born.

After lots of laughter, tears, notes and more notes, sewing sample after sample, suggestions from my students, and collaborations with my co-author and friend, Roberta Przybylski, the book is finally here! French is my native language, and I found the writing process laborious in English.

I first met Roberta at a couture fashion sewing center, where she was teaching classes and managing the shop. Following a stint as designer/manufacturer of earrings, Roberta returned to the sewing world and our partnership evolved. We combined my heirloom sewing background and Roberta's knowledge of sewing-machine skills and business savvy. With Roberta as the educational coordinator at our local sewing-machine store, we had the luxury of creating new classes, witnessing the success or failure of a particular project, and growing together in our belief that an heirloom quilt book was possible.

I knew I had a perfect fit with Roberta since her family had moved twelve times all over the United States and the world. Roberta also speaks another language, is a former school teacher, and has been teaching sewing for sixteen years. What a team we became! Her sewing knowledge, willingness to master her computer, and keen business sense proved to be an asset in focusing to meet our goal—a Victorian sampler quilt, with easy-to-follow directions, that you can make for your own family heirloom.

Yolande Fieson

THE HEIRLOOM QUILT

The sampler quilt featured in this book is composed of twelve different blocks, each using a different heirloom sewing technique. Step-by-step instructions guide you through the construction of each block. As you work on each block, we hope that you will come to love the feel and look of laces from another era as much as we do.

The quilt may look intricate but the sewing is easy, whether you are a beginner or an experienced sewer. Just follow the roses. One rose 🌹 indicates an easy block. Start with these, then move on to those marked with two roses 🌹🌹, which require intermediate skills. Those marked with three roses 🌹🌹🌹 are the most challenging. Try these after you have gained more skill and are ready for more advanced techniques. These symbols are found at the beginning of the directions for each block.

Although heirloom sewing (also called French hand sewing) was first executed by hand as a true art form, the instructions given in this book are geared to machine users. The quilt and the alternate projects shown in the photos can be completed with beautiful results by machine in a fraction of the time it normally would take by hand.

Before you start, read the "General Directions," beginning on page 7, to become familiar with heirloom sewing terminology. Feel free to tailor your project to your needs and skill level. You may decide to make just one square or multiples of only two or three of them to complete a twelve-block quilt. In addition to using the blocks for the sampler quilt, you can use the individual block designs for many other projects, including lingerie, linens, and clothing. Some of these uses are shown in the color photo section beginning on page 37. Directions are not included for these projects. They are meant for inspiration only.

Keep in mind that you are making an heirloom to be passed on to future generations. Don't hurry or feel overwhelmed. The Heirloom Quilt was designed to be completed in stages, block by block.

Take your time and learn new techniques in a leisurely fashion. Documenting your life, your children's lives, and the lives of their children in lace and batiste is truly worth your time and effort in this mobile, fast-paced society.

Making this quilt is also a great opportunity to share your sewing experiences with friends in the neighborhood. Setting aside one time a month for sewing will make the quilt a reality. For the new mother-to-be, timing the finishing of the quilt with her pregnancy might make the months go faster.

I wish Roberta and I could be there to hear firsthand about your sewing experiences over a four o'clock tea as my Maman did with her friends, but since that is not possible, we would love to see the results of your work. Please keep in touch by mail.

Yolande Filson
Roberta Przybylski

~ Cycles ~

Wedding bells are ringing
And we are late
I could not find the quilt
That my mother had made
It had fallen behind the piano in the parlor
I ran everywhere
Tripping on hoop skirts
Until little nephew George spied it
While playing with his wooden toys
My heart ceased its frantic knocking
As I rubbed my face upon the soft cotton
It is all that remains of her

My first child smiles up at me
From the depths of a draped bassinet
She is wrapped in downy billows of lace and trim
Her pacifier is a sodden quilt corner
The soft matting shielding her
From the mishaps of shaky first steps

Now she sleeps in a bed
Her chestnut curls captured by a velvet bow
She refuses to sleep without the quilt
It keeps the shadow demons away
Barricading them with trellises of lace

She has died
And so has my heart
The quilt smells of her childhood
Like clean straw
It drapes me with warmth
Yet I cannot sleep
When my eyes are closed
All I see are quilted pinwheels
Whirling crazily
When my eyes are open they lie flat
Tightly stitched down until my next dream

I have aged
So has the quilt
I cannot bear to look at it
It is banished to the attic

I am old
Tired of the junk I decide to sell it all
Halfway through an attic trunk I find it
A Victorian flag
Streaked and spotted with mildew
I wash it gently
Like a baby
I spread it on the summer grass to dry

Lying next to it I can hear
The faint beginning breaths of a newborn
One reborn

I have opened my own shop
The sign reads Antiques
But my living room is in the front window

Today she came
Timid
Small round red wrinkled baby
In the crook of her arm
Nothing interested her
Until she found it
She fingered the quilt

It is gilded with the thin sheen of age
A stitch for every wrinkle on my face
The appliquéd hearts and hands of generations past
This piece from the tablecloth stained with
Grandfather's coffee
A scrap from Mother's old brown dress
A cuff from the sleeve torn when sneaking over
    a farmer's fence
To taste the tang of green apples wet with twilight dew
I remember the parlor with its soft fishbowls of light
Falling from crystal lamps
The dark gleam of the mantle
The slippery scratchiness of the horsehair sofa
And the quilt draped over the piano

It unfurled in the young mother's hands
As she plucked at folds
Alive with lifetimes
Faded black buttons crouch on the cotton like beetles
Ribbons snake through slits
Licking at the borders with forked tongues
The threadbare corners are webbed with embroidery
Rosette spiders lurking underneath
They scuttle along the surface of the quilt
Peering at the baby

The mother turns to me
I can see what is in her eyes
The register reads NO SALE
As I wrap up the quilt for her

And so it begins again.

Chantal Lise Filson
Spring 1993

~ General Directions ~

*Y*ou will need special materials and basic sewing tools and supplies to complete your Heirloom Quilt. You will also need to know some sewing terminology that is basic to heirloom sewing techniques before you begin your first block. Please take the time to read this information carefully. A materials list appears on page 12.

FABRICS

The primary fabric in the Heirloom Quilt is batiste, but you will need a few other types of fabric for some of the blocks.

Batiste: Swiss cotton batiste is a finely woven fabric that comes in three different weights. The best quality is made in Switzerland, as the name implies, and is considered expensive in relation to similar domestic fabrics. It is hand washable. We used Nelona, a mid-weight Swiss cotton batiste, for the Heirloom Quilt. Imperial batiste is a cotton/polyester blend that is manufactured in the United States. It is washable and wrinkle-free and much less expensive than Swiss batiste. Although an attractive alternative, it does behave differently in the whip-and-roll technique used for the Heirloom Quilt. The polyester blend does not crease or roll easily. See page 12 for total yardage required to make this twelve-block quilt.

Organdy: You will need this crisp, sheer, fine cotton fabric for some of the blocks. Refer to the individual materials lists with each block. Organdy also makes a wonderful press cloth (below) because you can see through it so easily.

Assorted lace trims: See "Lace Trims" above right.

Cotton netting: This is used in the Victorian Attic Window block only. (See page 50.)

Muslin: Use a piece of this inexpensive, plain-weave fabric to cover your ironing board while working on your blocks. Wash it frequently to remove starch buildup, which can scorch and transfer to your work. You may substitute a clean white towel for the muslin.

Note: Batiste and the laces you will use are usually white, but you can alter the color if you wish with dye or a tea bath. Directions for tea dyeing appear on page 8.

LACE TRIMS

For centuries, lace has been associated with romance, wealth, and power. Handmade techniques gave way to machine-made finery when John Heathcoat perfected his loom in 1808 in the south of England. This innovative accomplishment made lace a more affordable commodity. From then on, looms across Europe produced fine-quality laces to adorn the homes and ladies of the Victorian era (1837–1900).

For this project, we chose laces and trimmings from various countries of origins. You will note that we incorporate many different laces and trimmings into the quilt blocks to add texture, interest, and artistic appeal. You may choose laces that have the same type of design motif if you prefer. However, you can be adventurous! Go for diversity and challenge yourself by gathering various laces, antique as well as new, and harmonizing them into one glorious celebration of your creative freedom of expression.

The basic guideline for choosing lace for your heirloom project is to use the required width, length, and type mentioned on the supply list for the block you are making. The lace pattern and style, however, remain your choice. Victorian women always had on hand an assortment of lace strips left over from previous projects. They incorporated these bits and pieces into their Crazy quilts.

The laces I chose for the Heirloom Quilt are machine-made of the finest natural fibers I could find. Hopefully, the quilt will be a family heirloom to be treasured by following generations. Buy the best you can afford. The trimmings used for this project are from England, France, and Switzerland.

English lace has an elaborate, open bobbin-work look. Cotton thread is used in the weaving process, which resembles tatting. *French lace* has a very intricate and delicate bobbin-work look with a netting background. It has a finer (100%) cotton thread but may have a 5%–10% nylon content, sometimes added for strength and durability. *Swiss embroidery* can best be described as machine-decorated strips of cotton batiste, stitched with matching or multicolored thread. These strips are usually 100% cotton and require care in pressing. The right side of the embroidery is raised and has a smooth feel and texture.

The following categories of lace trims are readily available in England, France, and Switzerland and in fabric stores in the United States.

Beading: A trimming with two straight edges and holes so you can thread narrow ribbon or cord through it.

Edging: A trimming with one straight edge (lace heading) and one scalloped edge.

Entre d'eux: Translated from the French, it means "between two." It is an embroidered batiste strip with the appearance of a miniature ladder and can be inserted between two strips of lace or batiste as a stabilizer.

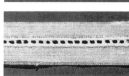

Galloon: A wide trimming with two scalloped edges.

Insertion: A trimming that has two straight edges (lace headings) so it can be sewn between other materials.

Medallion/Motif: A lace piece that is a recognizable design or motif, such as a heart or a basket, or an embroidered section with its own finished edge.

FABRIC PREPARATION

It is not necessary to preshrink lightweight batiste and laces of the same weight and fiber content before actually sewing the blocks. However, if the block contains fabrics, thread, and trims, with a mixture of different fibers, it is advisable to preshrink all items. They may shrink at different rates, resulting in some unwanted surprises in the completed quilt.

Place the lace and any other trim in a lingerie bag or colander when laundering. You can wash the completed blocks individually or after they have been assembled into a quilt top to remove any pencil marks. Follow the "General Laundering Directions" on page 72.

FABRIC DYEING

If you do not want a pristine white quilt, you may wish to add a delicate patina of "age" to the laces and batiste for your Heirloom Quilt. It is easy to do this since the cotton fabric and laces absorb color easily.

For a Victorian look, use either tea or coffee. Unfortunately, the directions cannot be as exact as if using a regular dye, which is another alternative. To prevent surprising results, test on a small fabric sample first.

Note: If this quilt will be used by a baby, pay special attention to any types of additives or chemicals.

Tea gives a softer hue with less yellow than coffee. The batiste used for the peach quilt on page 37 started out as baby pink, showing that you can make a dramatic difference with a little tea.

How to Tea Dye

1. Add 1 cup of white vinegar to 6 cups of water. This will help set the color.
2. Bring the solution to a boil, add 2 tea bags and allow to steep for 5 minutes. Place the solution in a metal or glass container, bowl, or pan.

Note: Do not use loose tea as a leaf might leave a small stain.

3. For even color absorption, wet the fabric thoroughly with cold water before placing it in the tea solution.
4. Immerse the unfolded, wet fabric into the tea solution. Do not allow the fabric to bunch as this will cause uneven color absorption, somewhat like tie dyeing. For a uniform color, smooth out the fabric in a single layer.
5. Have a clean white towel ready. After a few minutes, check the color, remembering that it will look darker when wet. When pleased with the color, immediately spread the yardage flat on a towel for drying. Roll and gently squeeze out the excess dye and water. If the color looks too dark, rinse in clear, cool water. Roll and squeeze again.

6. Press the damp fabric dry to remove wrinkles and heat-set the color.

Caution: Never allow the fabric to drip-dry as this will cause unevenness in the color.

Cotton and linen laces will take the tea dye in the same manner as the batiste. You can expect erratic and often disappointing results with those made from polyester or nylon.

TOOLS AND SUPPLIES

Before you start your quilt, make sure you have the following basic tools and supplies on hand.

Iron: You need a clean, reliable iron that does not leak, spit, or overheat. Make sure the sole plate is clean and free of starch and fusible-interfacing residue. For most work on this quilt, you will use a dry iron and spray starch. (See below.)

Towel: Use a clean white towel to cover the ironing board when starching or pressing. You can substitute a piece of muslin for the towel if you prefer.

Spray Starch: You will need a can of this with a fine mist spray. Since lace stretches easily and the batiste is soft, apply spray starch to add stability and aid in the sewing process. Always give the can a couple of shakes before spraying. Wait a few moments after spraying to allow the starch to be absorbed into the fabric. Press with a dry iron.

 Tip: If a finished piece of heirloom sewing must be stored away for a long period of time, it is best to launder the fabric to remove the starch. The glue properties in the starch tend to attract silverfish.

Sewing Machine: Make sure your zigzag sewing machine is clean and lint-free.

Presser Foot: Use an open-toe embroidery foot or a clear embroidery foot.

Bottom

Sewing-Machine Needles: Use a good-quality sewing-machine needle with a universal point, size #60/8.

Thread: Choose fine mercerized cotton thread, #60/2 or #50/2, usually referred to as an embroidery thread. You will also need regular sewing thread and embroidery floss for some

of the blocks. Refer to the materials lists for the individual blocks for specific requirements.

Marking Pencil: You will need a washout, chalk-type marking pencil and a sharpener. Our favorite is the Dixon brand. *Do not use fabric markers with disappearing ink* as the marks they make do not disappear entirely. In addition, the chemicals they contain are difficult to wash out and may do long-term damage to the fabric.

Measuring Tools: You will need a see-through ruler and a tape measure.

Pins: We prefer fine, steel-shaft pins with round heads for piecing, and flat-head flower pins from Clover for blocking and shaping.

Pinning Board: This is a padded surface on which you can shape lace and fabric. Directions for making one are on page 13.

Scissors: You will need a dressmaker's shears and an appliqué or sharp, double-pointed trimming scissors of the highest quality. Make sure they are sharp.

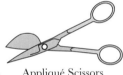
Appliqué Scissors

Rotary Cutter and Cutting Mat: You can use this circular cutting tool for speed and accuracy, as an alternative to conventional scissors. The mat protects the surface underneath from the cutting action.

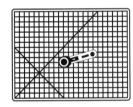
Rotary Cutter and Mat

Water-Soluble Stabilizer: Putting a small piece under the lace will keep the lace from disappearing into the throat-plate hole of your machine.

THE IMPORTANCE OF PRESSING

In the directions for each block, you will see the words "press" and "iron" listed in that order and you may wonder, "Is there a difference between pressing and ironing?" There certainly is!

To press (with either a steam or dry iron) means to apply and lift the hot iron from one location to another. When the sole plate is on the fabric surface, there is no sliding action, which prevents the fabric from shifting or becoming distorted. When directed to "press," repeat the above process again and again until the wrinkles disappear. After the fabric has been pressed, it is more stable and can withstand ironing.

Ironing is the process of moving the hot iron back and forth while the sole plate is in full contact with the surface to be smoothed. When wet or spray-starched, the fabric is weakened and ironing (without pressing first) may distort the grain line. This distortion changes both the shape and the way the fabric behaves.

Always press and iron in the direction of the fabric grain. Pretest the iron on a scrap of the lace or fabric for heat sensitivity before placing the iron on your actual work piece.

A Teflon-covered sole plate affixed to the heating surface of your iron helps prevent water spots and scorching. It also covers any burrs or other imperfections on the bottom of the iron that might damage delicate fabrics, and it glides easily over the surface of the fabric.

Use a Press Cloth

A sheet of white tissue paper, such as gift-wrapping tissue, makes a good press cloth. It is light, transparent, inexpensive, disposable, and works like a charm with a dry iron.

When using a steam iron, cotton organdy makes an excellent press cloth because its sheer, plain weave allows you to see your work easily. Pink the edges to control fraying.

As a rule, place your work right side down on a clean white towel or muslin and press from the back. The pile or nap of the towel helps prevent flattening of your embroidery stitches or any fabric texture.

BASIC CUTTING AND SEWING TECHNIQUES

There are a number of techniques that are necessary for many, if not all, of the blocks. First and foremost is cutting the pieces on grain.

Pulling a Thread

This procedure is essential for professional results and for finding the true crosswise grain of the fabric. Pulling a thread prevents fabric whiskers, and your finished work will look and hang better. For the Heirloom Quilt, it is not absolutely necessary to pull a thread for every batiste square; do so only when the directions tell you. If your fabric is a blend of natural and man-made fibers, clip the selvage and tear to find the true crosswise grain. For 100% cotton batiste, use the following method to find the crosswise grain line. Do not starch or press your fabric before you start.

1. Clip into the fabric selvage.

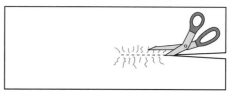

2. With a pin, pick up a thread about ½" (1.5cm) from the clipped edge and pull gently. Cut along the line made by the pulled thread.

If a thread breaks while you are pulling it, cut directly on the line left by the pulled thread and try to pick up the same thread a little farther down the puckered line. If unable to do so, pull the thread next to it.

For small sections or for fabric where selvages were cut away, pick up a thread in the center of the projected pull line. Place the needle into the thread loop and work from the center out.

Tip: After pulling on the thread, hold fabric and thread together; ease gathers down the line. This way, you place less stress on a single thread and it is not as likely to break.

Before cutting your batiste squares, refer to the cutting chart and layout diagram on page 14. You must follow the grain-line direction indicated to ensure consistency when cutting the required squares.

The crosswise grain has more give and stretches more readily than the lengthwise grain. You must cut everything on the same grain so that the finished quilt top and backing are compatible and will hang evenly.

Mark the lengthwise grain on each fabric piece at the outer edge as shown.

When you are ready to assemble the finished blocks into the quilt top, you will cut away the grain-line marking, since the squares for each block are cut oversized.

Mark the lengthwise grain with an arrow close to one outer edge of each piece.

Gathering Lace

If the block you are making requires lace gathering, *do not starch the lace*. The starch will fuse the lace threads together, making gathering very difficult. There is a gathering thread built into the heading of the lace. It is easily recognized as the loopy thread closest to the outside edge. Using a pin, loosen the first two or three loops, then gently pull the thread and evenly distribute the fullness. If you are working with a short lace strip, gather from both ends.

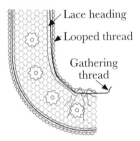

If the lace does not have a looped thread in the heading, pull the straight thread.

Lace heading
Looped thread
Gathering thread

Trimming

After sewing lace to batiste with a zigzag stitch as shown in the individual block directions, turn your work over to the wrong side and trim the fabric behind the lace in the following manner.

1. Hold the lace in a pinched fashion, using your thumb and index finger, and insert a pin in the fabric area that needs to be trimmed away.
2. Lift the pin to separate the batiste from the lace. Keeping the lace pinched, remove the pin and cut into the raised fold of the batiste. This will enable you to insert the pointed tip of the appliqué scissors between the two layers (lace and batiste) so you can start cutting without fear of poking a hole in your lace. Trim close to the zigzag stitching.

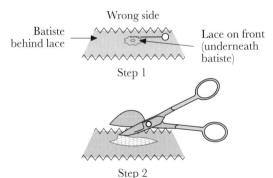

Wrong side

Batiste behind lace

Lace on front (underneath batiste)

Step 1

Step 2

Tip: Appliqué scissors are tremendously useful for any type of trimming. If you are afraid of cutting or nicking your lace, use rounded-tip scissors (similar to a child's scissors) as another option.

Oops, I Cut the Lace! What Do I Do Now?

Don't reach for a handkerchief and sob over your mishap! You can fix it.

1. Starch a piece of matching lace and place it under the cut area, carefully matching the lace pattern. You can also substitute cotton netting or organdy for a mending underlayer if necessary. Put a small piece of water-soluble stabilizer under the lace to keep the lace from disappearing into the throat-plate hole of your machine.
2. Set stitch width at 1 and stitch length at .25. Using the mending/serpentine or zigzag stitch, stitch the new lace in place.

Serpentine Stitch
SW 5;
SL 1

Zigzag Stitch
SW 2;
SL .5

3. Trim away the excess lace from the back side.

Tip: Appliqué a small lace motif to cover the mended area, such as a flower, bird, or butterfly. A friend embellished her quilt with miniature lace bow motifs that became the theme for the entire piece.

HEIRLOOM STITCHING BASICS

All seams are ¼"-wide (.75cm) unless otherwise noted. All stitches are given in metric for the European sewing machines. SL refers to stitch length and SW to stitch width (the space between the stitches from left to right).

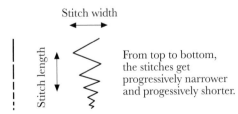

Stitch width

Stitch length

From top to bottom, the stitches get progressively narrower and progessively shorter.

If you own a domestic machine (Kenmore, Singer, etc.), follow the chart below to convert from the metric to inches.

SL .5 = 00 sts./inch	SL 2 = 12/14 sts./inch
SL 1 = 22 sts./inch	SL 2.5 = 10 sts./inch
SL 1.5 = 18 sts./inch	SL 3 = 8 sts./inch

Edgestitch: A straight stitch sewn along the outside seam or edge (SL 1.5 to 3).

Gathering Stitch: A long straight stitch used to shirr, ease, or gather in fullness (SL 3 to 5).

Hemstitching: Done with a wing needle to add special interest to hems and edges. It resembles entre d'eux and the Madeira stitch. For a more detailed explanation and illustration of this stitch, see the directions for the Grandmother's Fan block on page 55.

Mending/Serpentine Stitch: From time to time, this stitch is suggested as a substitute for the zigzag stitch. By following the recommended stitch width and stitch length, you can make your stitches blend into the lace netting while giving strength and stability. I love using this stitch to secure and reinforce a mitered corner in lace (SW 1; SL .5). This stitch is illustrated under "Oops! I Cut the Lace" on page 11.

Satin Stitch: A zigzag stitch (usually SW 1 to 3 and SL .5 or less). The stitches are very close together and resemble the buttonhole stitch.

Satin Stitch

Staystitch: Use as a basting stitch (SL 2 to 3). Staystitching helps prevent puckers, keeps lace from shifting, and makes zigzagging a quick, easy, and foolproof procedure. In most cases, you will staystitch the lace in place on the fabric square first, then zigzag over it. Staystitching by machine is an alternative to hand basting. If you ever have to undo a row of closely sewn zigzag stitches in heirloom sewing, you will discover how hard it is to see the fine stitching thread. It tends to blend in with the lace thread.

SAFETY FIRST

On some blocks, buttons are suggested as a decorative touch. If this quilt will be used on a baby bed as a bedcover, omit the use of all buttons and any loose ribbons. You may substitute a lace rosette, French knots, or other special hand stitches to add interest to the quilt.

If you do use buttons or charms on your blocks, apply a layer of clear nail polish to keep them from tarnishing and staining your work.

LET'S GET STARTED

The first step is to shop for the fabric and lace trims for your project. Listed below are the fabric requirements for the quilt. Refer to the supply list for the individual blocks for the types and amounts of lace required.

While you are shopping for your quilt materials, be sure to buy the materials required for making the Pinning Board. See page 13. Enjoy your shopping expedition!

Fabric Requirements

The Heirloom Quilt is made of four different layers. The top consists of the twelve blocks you will make first. Then you will add a layer of batiste, often a different color, such as peach, pink, or blue, under the assembled blocks. Beneath that is a layer of batting, followed by the backing, which is usually a piece of the same batiste used to make the blocks or the layer directly behind the blocks. The finished size of the completed quilt is approximately 39" x 49" (99cm x 124cm). The yardage requirements have been rounded up to allow for a little trial and error in your heirloom stitching.

Materials: 44"-wide (112cm) fabric

1¼ yds. (1.15m) Swiss cotton batiste for the blocks*

½ yd. (46cm) organdy for blocks

1½ yds. (1.4m) batiste for layer beneath finished blocks

1½ yds. (1.4m) batiste for quilt backing

43" x 53" piece of batting (109cm x 136cm)

*If you wish to use the same fabric for the blocks, the layer beneath the blocks, and the quilt backing, you will need 4½ yards (4m) of batiste.

Making a Pinning Board

Before you start to sew, take the time to make a pinning board. You will need to use this as a work surface for many of the blocks.

Materials

1 empty fabric bolt, approximately 7" x 22" (18cm x 56cm). Ask for one at your favorite fabric store.
1 piece of cardboard, approximately 11½" x 15" (30cm x 38cm), to use on top
12" x 16" (31cm x 41cm) piece of aluminum foil
½ yd. (46cm) cotton batting or polyester fleece
½ yd. (46cm) cotton muslin
1 piece of template plastic, 8½" x 11" (22cm x 28cm)
Clear, 2"-wide (5cm) adhesive tape commonly used for packing
Pins, needle, and thread
Serrated or X-acto® knife
Fabric glue stick or hot glue gun and glue

Directions

1. With a knife, cut the fabric bolt in half crosswise.

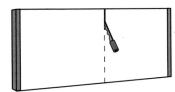

Empty fabric bolt

2. Place the halves together, side by side, with the uncut ends on opposite edges as shown. Tape together securely all around the center and across the edges. The resulting piece will measure approximately 11" x 14" (28cm x 36cm).

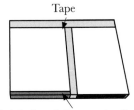

Tape

Fabric bolt ends in opposite directions

3. Cut the piece of cardboard to match the top of the joined sections. Position on top and tape in place. This piece covers any existing ridges in the taped board underneath.

4. Cut the aluminum foil slightly larger than the top surface of the board. The foil will act as a barrier so the cardboard won't collapse from the steam and as insulation to keep the heat of the iron from reaching the quilter's plastic template that you will place on the underside. (See step 9 below.)

5. Glue the foil to the board, with the excess wrapped down over the sides of the board. Tape the edges in place.

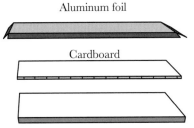

Aluminum foil

Cardboard

Fabric bolts taped together

6. With foil side down, lay the board on top of the fleece, with one long edge about 1" (2.5cm) from the edge. Tape the edge of the fleece to the board.

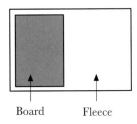

Board   Fleece

7. Wrap the fleece tautly around the board so that the front of the board (the side with aluminum) has two layers of fleece and the back only one layer.

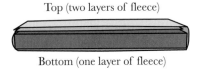

Top (two layers of fleece)

Bottom (one layer of fleece)

8. Trim away the excess fleece on one edge of the board. Pin, then hand stitch in place. Miter corners, pin in place, and whipstitch. Cover the board with muslin in the same way. The completed pinning board is the ideal size to use on your lap when you need a pinning surface during classes or while traveling, and it fits easily into a tote bag. Write your name and phone number on the end so you won't lose it if you leave it behind in class.

9. Use hot glue to attach an 8" x 11" (11cm x 28cm) piece of quilters' template plastic to the underside of the pinning board. This gives you a hard surface to work on when using a ruler and pencil to mark on your fabric.

Preparing Your Work Area

Because you will be working on light-colored, delicate fabrics, it is very important that your work area is clean as a whistle. Before you begin, do the following:

1. Clean your sewing machine and remove any lint left over from a previous project. Check the thread tension. If you do decide to oil your machine at this time, use a natural-fiber fabric, such as wool or cotton muslin, to absorb the excess oil residue. The thread in the needle should also be cotton for the same reason. This prevents oil from staining your delicate laces and batiste. Stitch through the fabric until no trace of oil is obvious.

2. When using spray starch, be sure to have a clean white towel or a piece of muslin available. Use it to cover your ironing board to avoid starch buildup, which can scorch and transfer to the fabric you are pressing.

3. Use a new needle in your sewing machine to help prevent skipped stitches and puckers in your fine batiste. *Always change the needle after eight hours of sewing.*

4. Clean your iron or change the water filter to avoid rusty leaks or residues from starch or interfacing. For the majority of your pressing needs, you will be using a dry iron along with the spray starch. When using steam, please make sure your iron is in good working order.

Cutting the Pieces

Follow the cutting layout below to cut the necessary pieces for each block. Be sure to mark the lengthwise grain line along the outer edge of each piece. Label and store the pieces in a clean, dry place until you are ready to use them.

A cutting list for each block appears in the box on page 15 for your reference.

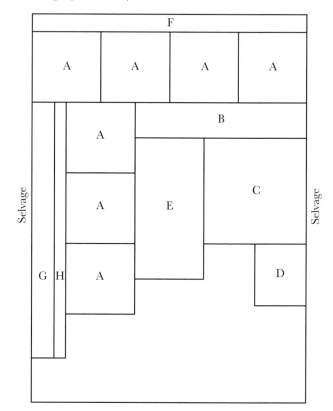

A. 11" square (28cm) for Grandmother's Fan, Heart, Bow, Heart in Hand, Log Cabin, All Tied-Up, Victorian Attic Window blocks
B. 6" x 27" (15cm x 69cm) for Pinwheel block
C. 15" square (38cm) for Trellis block
D. 7" x 11" (18cm x 28cm) for Log Cabin block
E. 11" x 20" (28cm x 51cm) for Basket of Points block
F. 2½" x 44" (6cm x 112cm) for Grandmother's Fan block
G. 2" x 27" (5cm x 69cm) for Rail Fence block
H. 1¾" x 27" (4.5cm x 69cm) Rail Fence block

BLOCK	FABRIC	
	Batiste	Organdy
Grandmother's Fan	11" square (28cm) 2½" x 44" (6cm x 112cm)	
Pinwheel	6" x 27" (15cm x 69cm)	
Heart in Hand	11" square (28cm)	11" square (28cm)
Rail Fence	1¾" x 27" (4.5cm x 69cm) 2" x 27" (5cm x 69cm)	
Crazy Quilt	Bits and pieces of textured fabrics	11" square (28cm)
Log Cabin	11" square (28cm) 7" x 11" (18cm x 28cm) (heavy batiste)	11" square (28cm)
Heart	11" square (28cm)	
Trellis	15" square (38cm)	
Basket of Points	11" x 20" (28cm x 51cm)	
All Tied Up	11" square (28cm)	
Attic Window	11" square (28cm)	11" square (28cm)
Bow	11" square (28cm)	
Total	1¼ yds. (1.15m)	½yd. (46cm)

Storing Blocks and Lace Leftovers

When you have finished each block, store it in a safe place until you are ready to assemble your quilt top. I use the following storage method.

1. Cover an empty paper towel or gift-wrapping tube with fleece or cotton flannel.
2. Place the completed block right side down on a piece of unbleached muslin.
3. Place the covered tube on top of the block and roll the layers around the tube, taking care to keep the block smooth and wrinkle-free.

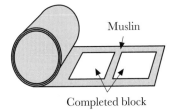

Muslin

Completed block

4. Use a safety pin to secure the muslin at both ends.

Note: Cut the strip of muslin long enough to accommodate all the blocks. As you finish each one, add it to the muslin and roll all of the blocks together on one handy storage cylinder.

Store starched lace leftovers on a small cardboard cylinder (paper towel or toilet-paper tube) covered with muslin. Fasten the lace ends with a rustproof safety pin to keep them from tangling.

A WORD OF ENCOURAGEMENT

While making a block, look upon it as a learning experience. Who has ever heard of anybody doing everything right the first time? Be kind to yourself!

❧ Heirloom Quilt Blocks ❧

🪷 Bow

Pioneer women used symbols found at home, in nature, or on the trail when they needed inspiration for their quilt blocks. The bow, used as an appliqué on a quilt, came to symbolize the steps in life's adventures. The path or direction of the bow is a series of twists and turns, ups and downs, but it is continuous, unbroken. Later, the bow was the inspiration for the Double Wedding Ring pattern with one difference— the beginning and the end were the same point in the design.

Techniques
Fold-Back Shaping
Lace Gathering for a Rosette

Materials

1 piece Swiss batiste, 11" square (28cm)
⅞ yd. (79cm) of ⅝"-wide (1.5cm) lace insertion
    for the bow
¼ yd. (23cm) of ¾"-wide (2cm) lace edging
    for the rosette
½ yd. (46cm) of ¹⁄₁₆"- to ⅛"-wide
    (3mm to 6mm) ribbon for the rosette
Optional: small button with shank* for
    center rosette

#60/2 fine cotton thread
#60/8 sewing-machine needle
Dixon washout chalk pencil
Spray starch
Pinning Board (See page 13.)
Appliqué scissors
Silk pins
Open-toe or clear machine-embroidery foot
Seam sealant, such as Fray Check™
Optional: 2" (5cm) square of water-soluble
    stabilizer

*If the quilt will be used by a baby rather than as a wall hanging, do not use a button. Securely bar-tack the rosette to the bow and cover the hole in the center of the rosette with the ribbon bow.

Preparation
Trace the pattern on page 19 onto a large sheet of white paper.

1. Mark the grain line along the outer edge of the batiste square.
2. Spray-starch and press the batiste and the lace insertion. *Do not starch the lace edging for the rosette.*
3. Fold the batiste square in half lengthwise with the grain; finger-press. Unfold.

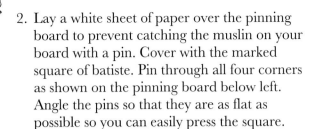

4. Fold the batiste in half on the crosswise grain and crease to mark the center.

5. Place the pattern for the bow on the pinning board.

6. Place the batiste square over the bow, matching the center crease to the center of the pattern. Pin through all layers—batiste, bow design sheet, and board—at the four corners to stabilize.

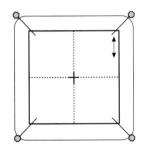

7. Using the washout chalk pencil, mark the dots (A–W) onto the batiste square. Unpin the batiste to remove the pattern.

Creating the Lace Bow

You may remember from your childhood the art of connecting dots to create a design. Use this same technique to complete the bow on your square of batiste, using the lace insertion and a technique called "Fold-Back Shaping." Be sure to follow the arrows in numerical order as you position, pin, and fold the lace insertion into the bow shape.

1. Place the bow design sheet on your work table in full view for easy reference. Also refer to block photo on page 38.

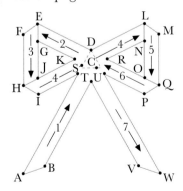

2. Lay a white sheet of paper over the pinning board to prevent catching the muslin on your board with a pin. Cover with the marked square of batiste. Pin through all four corners as shown on the pinning board below left. Angle the pins so that they are as flat as possible so you can easily press the square.

3. Referring to the pattern sheet, place the outer edge of the lace insertion at point A, allowing ¼" to extend below Point A. Pin at Point A, then follow the dots with the lace to Point D. Pin at Point D and Point B.

4. Fold the lace in the direction of arrow #2 and pin at Points E and C.

5. Fold lace in the direction of arrow #3 and pin at Points I and F.

6. Fold lace in the direction of arrow #4 and pin at Points L and H.

7. Fold lace in the direction of arrow #5 and pin at Points P and M.

8. Fold lace in the direction of arrow #6 and pin at Points D and Q.

9. Unpin at Point C.

10. Fold lace in the direction of arrow #7 and pin at Points W, S, and V.

11. Check to see that the lace is lying flat at all points. If not, unpin and repin as needed.

12. Finger-press the lace folds and pin through the lace edges at intersections—Points G, J, K, O, T, U, R, and N.

Sewing

1. Pin the lace bow into place by placing silk pins perpendicular to the lace headings every ½" (1.2cm). Remove the flat head pins. Transfer the batiste square with the lace bow to the sewing machine.

2. Set the machine for a stitch length of 2. Holding the top and bobbin threads together as you begin to sew, staystitch the bow to the batiste square. *Remove pins before you reach them.* If you nick the machine needle stitching over a pin, you will probably damage the lace and batiste with unsightly pulls. Stitch around the outside perimeter of the bow on the lace heading, across the bottom of the bow tails, and across the two inside bow triangles.

3. Machine stitch the small triangle at the center of the bow.

4. Fold back excess lace at the ends of the bow tails and trim even with angled ends.

5. With an open-toe or clear embroidery foot, zigzag (SW 2 and SL .5) over the staystitching and the bottom edge of each tail.

6. On the wrong side of the square, trim away the batiste behind the lace. See "Trimming" on page 11. *Do not trim behind the small center triangle* where the rosette will be attached.

Making the Lace Rosette

1. Use a pin to loosen the gathering thread at each end of the lace edging for about ¼" (6mm).

2. Fold the lace edging in half, matching the scalloped edges.

3. Straight-stitch (SL 2) about ⅛" (3mm) from the straight edge of the lace, keeping the gathering threads out of the way of the needle. If the lace tends to get pulled down into the hole in the throat plate of your machine, place a small piece of water-soluble stabilizer under your work.

4. Zigzag (SW 2; SL 1) over the straight stitching.

Straight-stitch, then zigzag.

5. Gently pull both gathering threads to form the rosette, leaving a small opening in the center to allow space for a shank button.

Knot the thread. Knot again and carefully apply a drop of seam sealant on the knots. Allow to dry and clip thread ends.

6. Tie a bow in the narrow ribbon and make a knot in each tail end.

7. Position the rosette at the center of the bow's lace triangle and pin. Hand sew rosette and button, if desired, in place.

Bow

E
F
L
M
G
D
N
2
4
3
5
K
R
S
C
J
T
U
O
4
6
H
I
P
Q
1
7
B
V
A
W
Creased line
Center
Lace placement

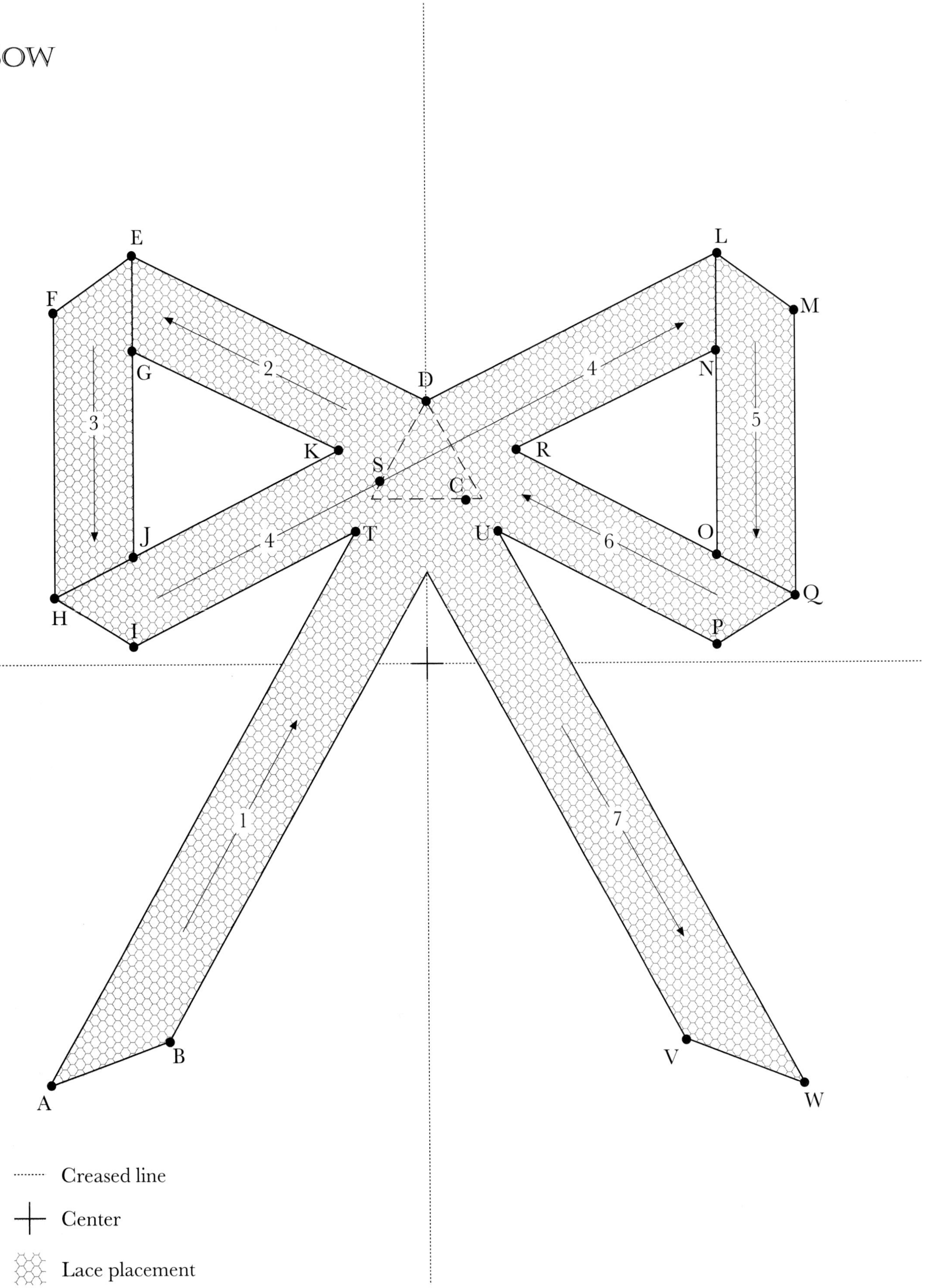

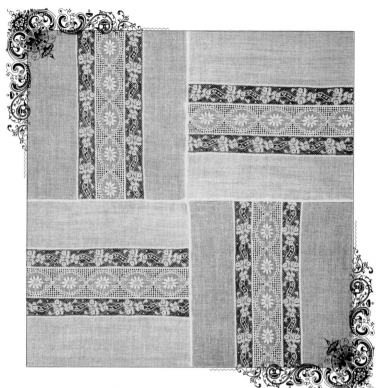

⚜ RAIL FENCE

*R*ail Fence is a traditional patchwork design and one of the easiest to do. In this interpretation, strips of batiste alternate with lace. Optical illusions formed with geometric blocks like the Rail Fence were more challenging and an alternative to the elaborate Crazy quilts of the Victorian era. During the Civil War, Rail Fence was called Railroad.

Techniques
*Butting Entre d'eux to Lace Insertion
Roll and Whip*

Materials
1 strip of Swiss batiste, 1¾" x 27" (4.5cm x 69cm)
1 strip of Swiss batiste, 2" x 27" (5cm x 69cm)
1½ yds. (137cm) of ⅝"-wide (1.5cm) French lace insertion
¾ yd. (69cm) Swiss embroidered insertion strip with entre d'eux edgings*; see illustration at right.
#60/8 sewing-machine needle
#60/2 fine cotton thread
Appliqué scissors
Rotary cutter, ruler, and mat
Spray starch

*It should be ⅞" wide (2.2cm), excluding the batiste seam allowance of the entre d'eux.

Preparation
Note: No pattern sheet is required for this block.

1. If you did not use a rotary cutter to cut the required pieces, use a pair of scissors to carefully trim away any "whiskers" on the edges.
2. Starch and press the batiste strips and lace.
3. Fold the French lace insertion in half crosswise and cut so you have 2 strips, each 27" (69cm) long. Set aside.
4. Trim away the batiste seam allowance that extends on each side of the entre d'eux edgings on the Swiss embroidery strip.

Sewing
1. Butt the Swiss embroidery and one French lace insertion strip next to each other as shown in step 3.
2. Hold the bobbin and top threads together and zigzag over the Swiss entre d'eux edge and the French lace heading (SW 2 and SL 1). (Don't worry if your stitching is not in every hole of the entre d'eux.)

3. Place the remaining strip of French insertion on the other side of the Swiss embroidery, matching the lace designs. If necessary, place the second strip so it is a mirror image of the first one. Zigzag as you did the first strip.

Approximately 2⅛"

Mirror Image

4. Spray-starch, press, and iron (pages 9–10) the assembled strip. At this point, your sewn strip should be approximately 2⅛" (5.4cm) wide.

Roll and Whip

1. Place the prepared lace strip on top of the 1¾" x 27" (4.5cm x 69cm) batiste strip with right sides together and the long cut edge (not the selvage edge) of the batiste strip extending ⅛" (3mm) beyond the right-hand edge of the lace.

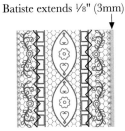

Batiste extends ⅛" (3mm)

2. Hold bobbin and top threads together and zigzag (SW 3.5 and SL 1) over the extended batiste edge and the lace heading. Make sure that the needle stitches into the lace on every left-hand swing of the needle and that it clears the extended edge of the batiste on every right-hand swing. You will see the batiste roll over the lace heading.

Rolled edge after stitching

⅛" (3mm)

Roll and Whip

3. Repeat steps 1 and 2 on the remaining edge of the lace, using the 2" x 27" (5cm x 69cm) strip of batiste. Press the seams on the wrong side, then press the rolled seams toward the batiste strips from the right side. Spray-starch, press, and iron.

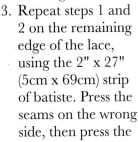

Press toward batiste.

4. Using rotary-cutting tools, square off and trim one end of the assembled strip.

5. Measure the finished width of the strip. It should be about 5¼" to 5¾" (13.2cm to 14.6cm) wide.

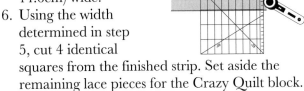

Square off corner.

6. Using the width determined in step 5, cut 4 identical squares from the finished strip. Set aside the remaining lace pieces for the Crazy Quilt block.

7. Position the squares as shown with the narrower batiste strip in each square toward the center of the larger square you are forming.

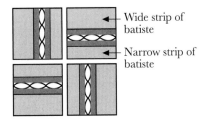

Wide strip of batiste

Narrow strip of batiste

8. Sew squares together in sets of 2, using the roll-and-whip technique (zigzag: SW 3.5 and SL 1). Place the square with the long strip of batiste on the bottom and the one with the lace edge on top while stitching. Spray-starch and press.

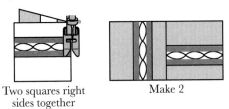

Two squares right sides together

Make 2

9. Pin the 2 sets of blocks together, matching the center seams. Using the roll-and-whip technique, stitch the seam as described in step 8. Spray-starch, press, and iron.

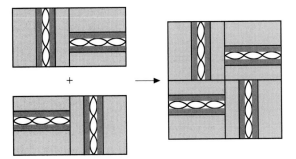

+

♫ Heart in Hand

This pattern is an interpretation of the old Shaker folk design. The Heart in Hand design symbolizes love, friendship, and the art of giving. When money and materials were scarce, women used their hands as tools. In the kitchen, they would place one hand over pressed cookie dough while the other hand would cut around it.

The shape of the loving heart has been a recurring design on many quilts for a long time. This block is an opportunity to put your own hand print on this Heirloom piece.

An old Victorian inscription for this design reads:

Hand and heart shall never part,
When this you see,
Remember me . . .

Techniques
Reverse Appliqué
Lace Gathering
Lace-Motif Application

Materials
1 piece dotted Swiss batiste, 9" square
   (23cm x 23cm), for the hand
1 piece Swiss batiste, 11" square (28cm x 28cm)
1 piece cotton organdy, 11" square (28cm x 28cm)
¼ yd. (23cm) of 2"-wide (5cm) lace edging
   or galloon
1 lace heart motif, approximately 1¾" x 2"
   (4.5cm x 5cm)

#60/2 fine cotton thread
#60/8 sewing-machine needle
Masking tape
Appliqué scissors
Spray starch
Open-toe or clear machine-embroidery foot
Dixon washout chalk pencil
Optional: 2" (5cm) square of water-soluble
   stabilizer
Optional embellishment supplies:
   Miniature baby pacifier or other charm
     of your choice
   1 yd. (1 meter) of narrow silk ribbon
   Large-eyed needle with sharp point
   Lace bird motif

Preparation
Note: No pattern sheet is required for this block.

Be sure to mark the grain line on the edge of all the squares (page 10). When layering the squares during the construction process, make sure grain lines are going in the same directions, and when overlapping layers, match the grain-line direction.

1. Spray-starch, press, and iron the dotted Swiss and the batiste squares on both sides.

2. Lay the dotted Swiss batiste right side down on a hard surface. Tape in place around the outside edge to stabilize. See illustration with step 3 on page 23.

Note: The directions that follow will produce a finished block with a right hand. The photo on page 22 shows a left-hand block.

3. Center your hand on the wrong side of dotted Swiss square and trace around it with the Dixon pencil. Draw a line across the bottom edge of the hand outline to complete the hand. Remove the tape.

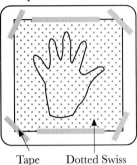

Tape   Dotted Swiss

Tip: If your hand is too large for a square that finishes to 9¾" (25cm), substitute someone else's hand—baby's or grandmother's, for example. For sentimental reasons, you may wish to appliqué your wedding glove or Holy Communion glove instead of a dotted Swiss hand. If so, appliqué to the batiste square and disregard the instructions for making the hand below.

4. Fold the Swiss batiste square in half lengthwise and finger-press. Unfold. Place the traced hand, wrong side up, on the wrong side of the batiste, and leave enough space at the bottom to accommodate the lace cuff. Pin all layers together.

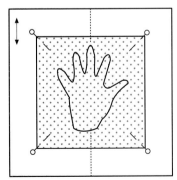

Sewing

1. Replace the regular presser foot with an open-toe or clear embroidery foot. Set the machine for a zigzag stitch (SW 1; SL 1).

2. Zigzag over the marked outline of the hand, pivoting as shown. Remove the pins.

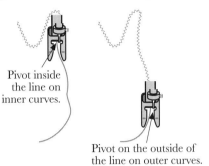

Pivot inside the line on inner curves.

Pivot on the outside of the line on outer curves.

3. Trim away the excess dotted Swiss around the outer edge of the hand.

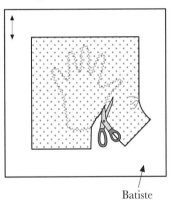

Batiste

4. Turn the work over to the right side and carefully trim away the batiste to expose the right side of the dotted Swiss. This is called working on the edge.

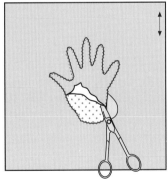

Right side
Trim batiste to expose dotted Swiss.

5. Place the completed hand right side up on the organdy square and pin together, matching grain lines. Zigzag (SW 2; SL .5) all the way around the edge of the hand, covering the first row of stitching. Staystitch (SL 2) ¼" (6mm) from the outer edges of the block.

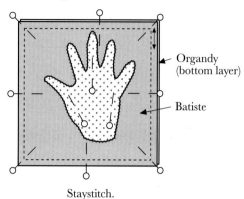

Staystitch.

Adding the Lace Motif and Cuff

1. Position the heart motif in the palm of the hand and zigzag (SW 1.5; SL 1) all the way around the edges.
2. On the ¼-yard piece of lace edging, undo 2 to 3 thread loops of the gathering thread in the heading. Draw up, gathering the lace to fit the bottom edge of the hand. (See page 11.)
3. Zigzag (SW 1.5; SL 1) over the raw edges of the lace, placing a small piece of water-soluble stabilizer under the lace to prevent it from being pushed into the throat-plate hole. Remove the stabilizer. Set aside the lace cuff

to apply to the hand after the quilt has been assembled and washed.

4. To sew the cuff to the hand, pin in place, turning under the lace ends. Stitch in place by hand.

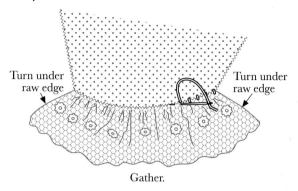

Gather.

Adding the Embellishments

Add all embellishments after the block has been laundered. Refer to the block photo on page 38.

1. Thread narrow ribbon into a large-eyed needle. Tie the pacifier to the ribbon, leaving a 4"-long (10cm) tail. Weave the ribbon in and out of the outstretched fingers. Do not pull the ribbon taut; loops should form around the fingers. Secure the loops with French knots. Tie a knot at each end of the ribbon.
2. Pin the bird motif in the upper corner of the block between the thumb and the index finger. Position ribbon under the bird's beak. Zigzag (SW 1; SL 1) over the edges of the motif.

⚘ ⚘ LOG CABIN

This is a lacy interpretation of the classic Log Cabin patchwork design that symbolizes the warmth and hospitality of early-American family life. The embroidered piece in the middle replaces the traditional red center section. This red center represented the fireplace, which was in the heart of the home. Quilters who lived along the seashore often used yellow in the center to signify a lantern illuminating the window of the log cabin at night—a beacon to help their loved ones at sea find their way home.

The use of satin and velvet ribbons identifies the Straight Furrows or Ribbon variation of the Log Cabin. It is named for its resemblance to the narrow trenchlike furrows created by the plow in the farm fields. Victorian women often added a lace edging around the quilt to complement and, at the same time, contrast with the rich colors and textures of the pieced quilt.

Traditionally, the Log Cabin block was pieced with alternating light and dark fabric strips to depict the sunlight and shadows on the logs of the house. The contrast between the light and dark color values in this block is usually well defined, thus providing a variety of possibilities for block assembly. For the Heirloom Quilt, you will be working with materials of the same color, so it is important to use two different types of material— lace insertion and Swiss embroidery—to add subtle definition to the finished block.

Techniques
Lace Butting
Flat-Lace Application

Materials

1 piece of Swiss batiste, 11" square (28cm)
1 piece of cotton organdy, 11" square (28cm)
1 piece of embroidered cotton, 2" square (5cm)*
1 yd. (92cm) of ⅝"-wide (1.5cm) French lace
    insertion for outer corners of block
1 piece of batiste or lawn, 7" x 11" (18cm x 28cm)
French or English lace insertion
    Row 1: ⅝" x 6" (1.5cm x 15cm)
    Row 2: ⅝" x 9" (1.5cm x 23cm)
    Row 3: ⅝" x 12" (1.5cm x 31cm)
Swiss embroidery strips with entre d'eux edgings
    Row 1: ⅝" x 8" (1.5cm x 21cm)
    Row 2: ⅝" x 10" (1.5cm x 26cm)
    Row 3: ⅝" x 13" (1.5cm x 33cm)
#60/8 sewing-machine needle
#60/2 fine cotton thread
Appliqué scissors
Open-toe or clear machine-embroidery foot

*Use a section of an embroidered handkerchief or a square motif of Swiss embroidery.

Preparation

Use pattern on the pullout pattern sheet.

1. Mark the grain line on the edge of each fabric square. (See page 10.)
2. Spray-starch and press the batiste, lace strips, and center motif; set aside.
3. Trim away the batiste seam allowance next to the entre d'eux edges on the Swiss embroidery strips.

Entre d'eux

4. Fold the 6" (15cm) piece of lace insertion in half and cut into 2 pieces, each 3" (7.5cm) long. Label each piece 1L (L for lace).
5. Fold and cut the 9" (12cm) piece of lace insertion into 2 equal lengths and label each 2L. Do the same with the 12" (16.5cm) piece and label 3L.
6. Repeat this procedure for the entre d'eux from the Swiss embroidery pieces. Fold, cut, and label 1E, 2E, and 3E (E for embroidery).

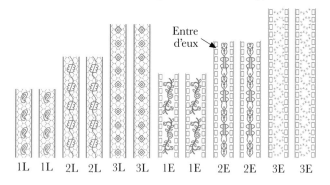

Entre d'eux

1L 1L 2L 2L 3L 3L 1E 1E 2E 2E 3E 3E

7. Fold the organdy square in half lengthwise and finger-press the crease. Unfold. Fold the organdy in half crosswise and finger-press the crease. Unfold.
8. Place the embroidered center motif on the diagonal in the center of the organdy square so that the corner points line up with the creased lines. Pin in place.

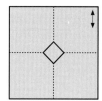

Sewing

1. Staystitch (SL 2) the center piece in place about ⅛" (3mm) from the outer edges.

2. Position lace piece 1L on top of the organdy, right side up, lapping the lace heading ¹⁄₁₆" (1.5cm) over the unfinished edge of the center motif. Allow ⅛" (3mm) of lace to extend above the top edge of the motif. Stitch (SL 2) the lace headings (both finished edges) in place, stitching ⅛" (3mm) past the bottom edge of the lace center piece. Fold the lace strip back onto itself and carefully trim away the excess. At least ⅛" (3mm) of lace should extend beyond the bottom edge of the center piece after trimming.

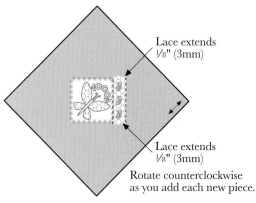

Lace extends ⅛" (3mm)

Lace extends ⅛" (3mm)

Rotate counterclockwise as you add each new piece.

Note: If using a medallion with a finished edge, stitch just inside the finished edge and butt the lace pieces up to the finished edge as you add them. This procedure will give you a slightly larger Log Cabin piece without interfering with the block-assembly process. Don't worry, you have sufficient lace to complete your Log Cabin square.

3. Zigzag (SW 1.5; SL 1) over the first row of stitching on the inside lace headings.

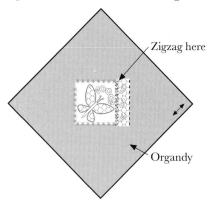

Zigzag here

Organdy

4. Rotate the block counter-clockwise and place the remaining 1L piece along the next side of the center piece with ⅛" (3mm) extending above the top edge as before. Use a straight stitch and then zigzag in place as you did the first piece. Trim, leaving a ⅛"-long (3mm) tail beyond the bottom edge of the center piece as you did with the first piece of lace.

Extending ⅛" (3mm)

Extending ⅛" (3mm)

Tip: Keep your work neat by clipping threads as you go.

5. Turn the block counterclockwise again and place strip 1E on the next side of the center motif as before. Staystitch (SL 2) the Swiss embroidery strips on the inside edge of the entre d'eux, then zigzag (SW 1.5; SL 1) the edges in place. Add the remaining 1E strip in the same manner.

6. Continue rotating and building the block by adding 2 strips of lace (L) and then 2 strips of Swiss embroidery (E) as you work around the center piece. There should be 3 rows of each on the block as shown in the block illustration above right.

7. Zigzag (SW 2; SW 1) over the outer edge of the last pieces added, including the short, cut ends.

8. Place the block face down on a towel-covered ironing board and press.

9. With the right side of the block facing up, place the 7" x 11" (18cm x 28cm) piece of batiste under the half of the block made with Swiss embroidery strips. The inner edge should extend past the center of the center piece in the Log Cabin (indicated by dashed line in illustration). Pin in place. Zigzag (SW 1.5; SL 1) over the outer and inner edges of the Swiss embroidery pieces and the edge of the center piece as shown.

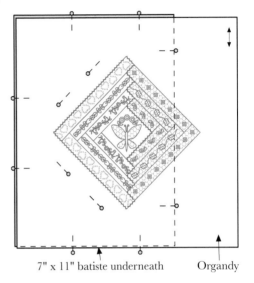

7" x 11" batiste underneath   Organdy

10. On the wrong side of the block, trim away the excess batiste close to the zigzagging. Press.

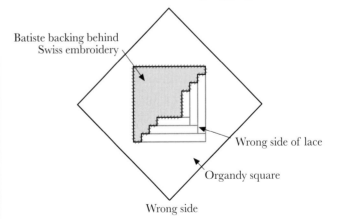

Batiste backing behind Swiss embroidery

Wrong side of lace

Organdy square

Wrong side

Corners

1. Draw a line 1" (2.5cm) from the edge of the last row of the Log Cabin strips on all 4 sides of the block. Place the edge of a piece of lace insertion along the line and pin in place. Staystitch (SL 2) in place in the lace headings on each side of the lace. Trim excess lace even with the block edges.

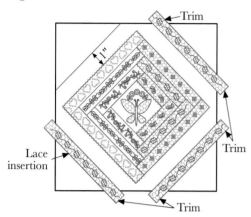

Do not trim away the organdy under these lace strips.

2. Place the Log Cabin block on top of the 11" (28cm) square of batiste, matching grain-line directions. Pin in place. Zigzag (SW 2; SL 1) over the outer heading on each piece of lace.

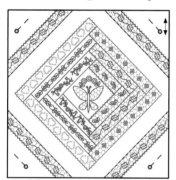

3. On the wrong side of the block, carefully trim away the batiste center along the zigzagging on the inner heading of each piece of lace insertion. The resulting block will then have 1 layer of batiste and 1 layer of organdy in each outer corner triangle.

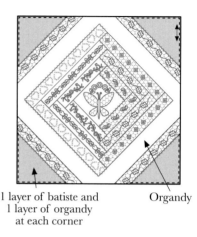

1 layer of batiste and 1 layer of organdy at each corner   Organdy

4. Staystitch (SL 2) ¼" (6mm) from the outer edge of each corner triangle as shown in the illustration above. Press from the back.

✄ ✄ TRELLIS

*T*his block is a lacy version of a traditional *Ninepatch* quilt block. It requires a lace-mitering technique that takes me back down memory lane to my days in couture design school. In our class for a Chanel-style jacket, we added trim, mitering corners in much the same way you will learn to miter the lace in this block. Over the years, I have found that this method gives me the most professional finish. With a few minor changes, I adapted the technique for heirloom sewing.

To personalize your quilt, you can embroider flowers, the baby's name, and the birth date in the trellis squares. When embroidering by machine or by hand, remember that the trellis square is very delicate. Be careful to leave batiste behind the laces until after the work is completed. Family members can autograph in the squares with a permanent fabric pen to commemorate baby's happy arrival. Test on a batiste fabric scrap first.

Techniques
Lace Insertion Seaming
Lace Mitering

Materials
1 piece of Swiss batiste, 15" square (38cm square)
1⅝ yds. (152cm) of ⅜"-wide (1.5cm) French or
    English lace insertion
#60/2 fine cotton thread
#60/8 sewing-machine needle
Heavy spray starch
Dixon washout chalk pencil
Open-toe or clear machine-embroidery foot
Silk pins
Pinning Board (See page 13.)
Ruler
Appliqué scissors
Optional: permanent ink fabric pen

Preparation
Trace the pattern on page 32 onto a large sheet of white paper.

1. Mark the grain-line direction on the edge of the batiste square. Spray-starch, press, and iron the batiste and lace insertion.
2. Fold the batiste square in half lengthwise and finger-press. Unfold. Fold batiste in half crosswise and finger-press. Unfold.
3. Place the pattern design sheet over the pinning board and lay the batiste square on top, lining up the creases with the crease-line marks on the pattern. Pin in place at all 4 outer corners of the batiste.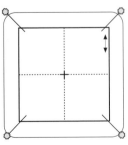
4. Mark all the dots, A–H, and numbers 1–4. Unpin and set pattern aside.

5. Place the batiste on a hard, smooth surface and use a ruler to draw the 4 lace placement lines (the bold lines marked with letters). Connect A to B, C to D, E to F, and G to H. Do not connect the numbered dots yet. To avoid line distortion, press firmly on the ruler while drawing the lines. Transfer the marked batiste back to the pinning board.

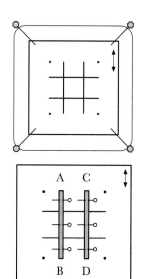

6. Center lace insertion over line AB. Pin in place and cut away excess lace. Repeat on line CD, matching the placement of the lace design to the placement in the first piece.

Sewing

1. Staystitch (SL 2.5) in the lace headings on each lace strip. Sew in the same direction from top to bottom.

2. Turn the work over and cut the batiste under the lace on the marked lines to the lettered points, also cutting across the width of the lace insertion at the top and bottom. *Do not cut the batiste away.*

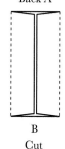

Back A

B
Cut

3. Fold the batiste back toward each lace heading and finger-press. From the right side, zigzag (SW 2; SL .5) over the lace headings. Trim excess batiste close to the zigzagging on the back.

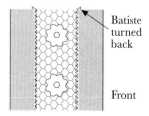

Batiste turned back

Front

4. Center lace over line EF, pin in place, and trim excess lace. Repeat with line GH, making sure to match the lace motifs to those in piece EF. Staystitch, fold, cut, zigzag, and trim as you did with the first 2 pieces of lace. At this point, your work should look like a tic-tac-toe board game.

5. From the back, spray-starch, press, and iron. On the front of the work, use a ruler to connect the dots from corner to corner to form a square. (See illustration below.)

Mitering the Corners

1. Heavily starch and press the lace insertion.

2. Place the trellis pattern on the pinning board with the tic-tac-toe square on top. Center the square, matching the dots at the 4 corners. Pin through all layers (batiste, pattern, and pinning board), placing pins outside the trellis design at all 4 corners to stabilize it.

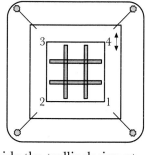

Note: To make steps easier to see, lace pattern is not shown in the following illustrations.

3. Starting at corner #1, place lace insertion over the lace placement area, with the end of the lace extending ½" (1.25cm) past the corner. Place a pin through the lace heading at the dot where outside corner #1 and the inside lines intersect.

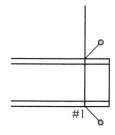

#1

4. With lace held in position, take lace to corner #2, being careful not to stretch the lace. Pin through the lace heading at corner #2. Fold the lace back onto itself and pin at point D to keep it in place and out of the way while you fold the first mitered corner.

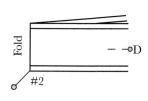

Fold
#2
D

5. At corner #2, turn the folded edge of lace back on the diagonal with the straight folded edge just short of the outside lace heading. Finger-press.

6. Unfold the diagonal corner. Weave a fine silk pin through the creased line.

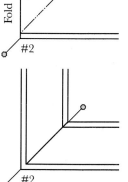

Fold
#2

7. Remove the pin at D and take the lace to corner #3. Pin, then fold and press the miter as you did at corner #2. Repeat for corner #4.

8. After completing corner #4, take the lace back to corner #1. Remove the pin at point #5, where the lines intersect, and repin through the 2 lace-strip headings.

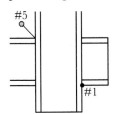

9. Fold the top lace tail under at a 45° angle so the 2 lace tails are even as shown. Unpin at corner #1, then pin through both lace headings. Finger-press the fold.

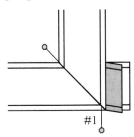

10. Place pins across the folded edge.

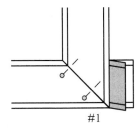

11. Remove pins at all 4 corners of the lace, *leaving only those holding the mitered folds in the lace.* Mark the position of each of the 4 inside corners with a dot on the lace. The mitered lace should now be totally free from the batiste.

12. Transfer the lace to the sewing machine. Very carefully, unpin corner #2. Place the lace under the presser foot with a small piece of water-soluble stabilizer underneath. Hold your bobbin and top threads together as you sew a straight stitch (SL 1.5) on the crease line from the inner corner to the outer corner. Do not cut threads yet.

13. Lift the presser foot, turn the lace over, and zigzag (SW 2; SL 1) on top of the first row of stitching. When you open out the completed corner, the lace heading should turn a perfect corner on the outer edge. Trim away the stabilizer.

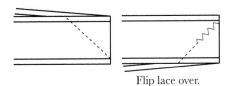

Flip lace over.

14. Sew the next 2 mitered corners in the same manner.

15. At the last corner (corner #1), edgestitch (SL 1.5) through all layers of the lace along the folded edge. Leave the needle in the lace, pivot, and zigzag (SW 1, SL .5) or serpentine stitch (SW 1; SL .5) over the edgestitching.

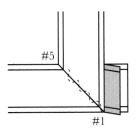

16. Pin the mitered lace over the batiste to check the fit. Pin in place at the 4 corners. Adjust the fit if necessary.

17. Remove the lace from the batiste; trim away the excess lace from the corner mitered seams.

18. Pin the lace to the batiste. Staystitch (SL 2.5) in the lace heading on the outer edge of the lace square. Repeat on the inner heading. Zigzag (SW 2; SL .5) over the staystitching.

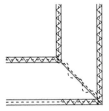

19. Carefully trim away the batiste behind the lace (page 11). Spray-starch, press, and iron the completed trellis from the back.

20. For additional strength, zigzag or serpentine stitch (SW 1; SL .5) over the mitered seam at corners 2, 3, and 4.

TRELLIS

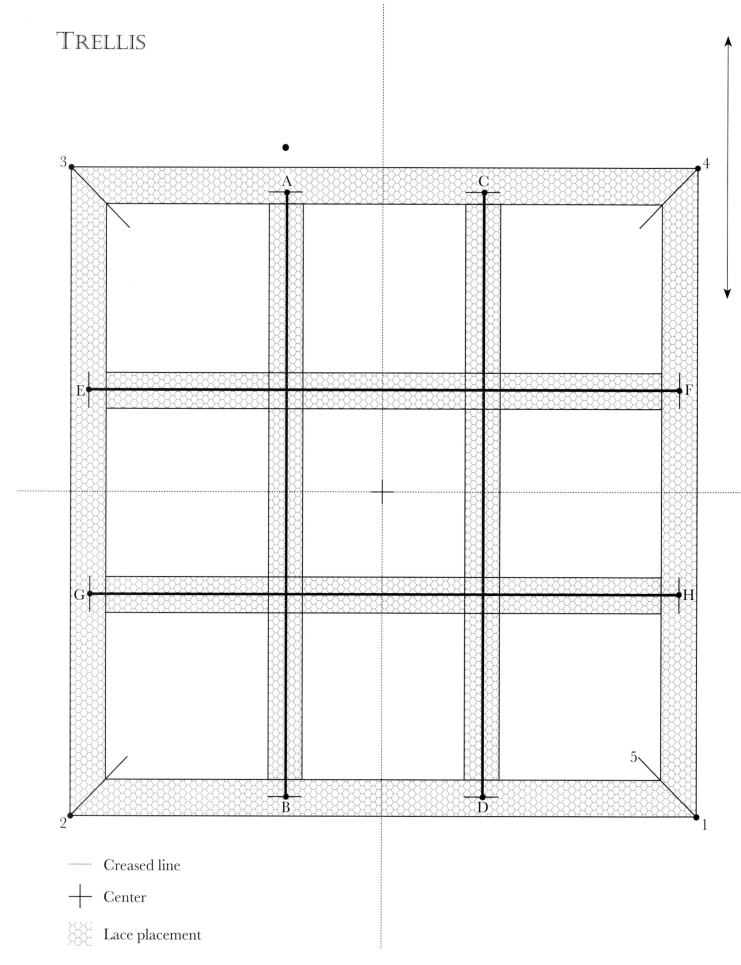

Creased line

Center

Lace placement

♫ ♫ ALL TIED UP

All Tied Up is a remembrance of something from my childhood. Although not truly based on a traditional patchwork block, it has its roots in the same thrifty and saving nature that prompted patchwork.

Since I was the eldest girl in the family with one older brother and three younger sisters, the majority of my clothes were new. What a privilege! Maman would sew many tucks in the skirt and sleeve sections of my clothes, and as I grew, she would undo a tuck or two. As the garment was handed down from one sister to another, the folded edge of the tucks would become worn, leaving a noticeable line. My mother would undo the tuck, cut directly on the threadbare area, and insert a lace or ribbon strip.

My youngest sister, Rollande, was actually the privileged one because she received the garment last, and by that time it had the maximum amount of fancy trimming. Wherever there was a stain or a tear, a lace motif was appliquéd or a flower was embroidered to cover the mishap. The garment may have been older but it certainly looked better.

You can personalize your square with machine or hand embroidery. If your project will be a baby gift, write the baby's name and birth date on the ribbon in the center of the piece. A fine rayon embroidery thread works best because the shine will enhance the ribbon. It's best to use thread in a darker shade of the same color used for the ribbon. A Pigma pen or other permanent pen can be used in place of machine stitching for personalizing. Practice first on scrap fabric or ribbon.

Technique

Lace Butting
Fold-Over Mitering

Materials

1 piece Swiss batiste, 11" square (28cm)
1 yd. (92cm) of ¾"-wide (2cm) lace insertion
1 yd. (92cm) of ½"-wide (1.25cm) lace insertion
1 yd. (92cm) entre d'eux, medium width
½ yd. (46cm) of ⅜"-wide (9mm) lace beading
½ yd. (46cm) of ⅛"-wide (3mm) satin ribbon
    to weave through the beading
¼ yd. (23cm) of 1"-wide (2.5cm) double-faced
    satin ribbon for the block center
1 yd. (92cm) of ¼"-wide (6mm) double-faced
    satin ribbon for outer edges of square
1 skein cotton embroidery floss (DMC)
Tapestry needle, size 14
Appliqué scissors
Fabric glue stick
#60/2 fine cotton thread
#60/8 sewing-machine needle
#75/11 machine-embroidery needle for
    embroidering center ribbon
Heavy spray starch
Pinning Board (See page 13.)
Optional: 2" (5cm) of water-soluble stabilizer
Optional: edgestitching foot or a foot with a
    separating bar
Open-toe or clear machine-embroidery foot

Dixon washout chalk pencil
Rotary cutter and mat
Ruler
Optional: button, lace rosette, or charm

Preparation

Trace the pattern on page 45 onto a large sheet of white paper.

1. Embroider the center ribbon as desired.
2. Mark the grain line at the outer edge of the batiste square. (See page 10.)
3. Spray-starch, press, and iron the laces, entre d'eux, and the batiste square.
4. Place the pattern in full view so you can refer to it for strip placement.
5. Lay the 1"-wide (2.5cm) satin ribbon over the center ribbon placement on the pattern. The ribbon will be longer than needed.
6. Trim away the batiste seam allowance on 1 edge of the entre d'eux. Fold in half crosswise and cut into 2 equal lengths. Set aside.

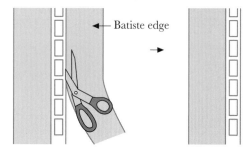

← Batiste edge

7. Cut the ½"-wide (1.25cm) lace insertion into 2 equal lengths. Set aside.

Sewing

1. Place a 2" (5cm) square of water-soluble stabilizer under the presser foot of your sewing machine to keep the lace from disappearing into the hole in the throat plate.
2. Set the machine for zigzag stitching (SW 2; SL 1). Replace the regular presser foot with an edgestitching foot if you have one for your machine.
3. Place the end of 1 trimmed piece of entre d'eux right side up on top of the stabilizer with the batiste to the left. Place a piece of ½"-wide (1.25cm) lace insertion to the right of and

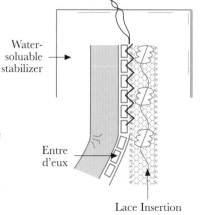

Water-soluable stabilizer

Entre d'eux

Lace Insertion

next to the "holes" of the entre d'eux. The edges should butt, not overlap. You are ready to use the "butting" technique to sew adjoining strips together.

4. Holding the top and bobbin threads together, begin zigzag stitching over the edges of the entre d'eux and the lace. The needle should go into the holes of the entre d'eux, but it is OK if you miss a hole occasionally or stitch into one of the bars in the entre d'eux.

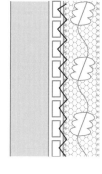

5. Trim away the batiste seam allowance on the other side of the entre d'eux. Align the edge of the other piece of the lace insertion on the remaining edge of the entre d'eux. *Make sure to position the lace motifs so they are a mirror image of those in the first piece of lace insertion.* Zigzag stitch as you did the first piece. Cut away the stabilizer behind the lace.

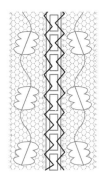

Motifs in lace insertion on each side of entre d'eux should be mirror images.

6. Cover the ironing board with a white towel or muslin. Spray-starch and press the butted lace strip.

7. Sew the remaining piece of entre d'eux to the butted lace strip. Trim away the remaining batiste. Fold the resulting piece in half crosswise and cut into 2 equal lengths.

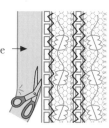

Batiste →

Lace Insertion

8. Cut the ¾"-wide (2cm) piece of lace insertion into 2 pieces of equal length. Butt and zigzag stitch a piece of insertion to each side of the lace beading. Press after the first stitching to eliminate any distortion. Spray-starch and press the finished piece. Allow to cool.

Beading

9. Fold the lace/beading strip in half crosswise and cut into 2 equal lengths. Butt and stitch each piece to 1 of the lace/entre d'eux pieces. Each resulting piece should be approximately 2¾" x 9" (7cm x 23cm).

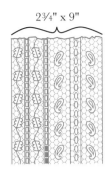

2¾" x 9"

10. Butt and stitch a lace insertion/beading/entre d'eux strip to each side of the center ribbon.

Ribbon

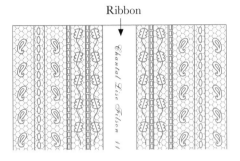

11. Before pressing, make sure that the excess water-soluble stabilizer has been trimmed away. Turn the work over with the right side against the towel-covered ironing board. Spray-starch and press from the back.

Cutting

1. Using rotary-cutting equipment, square off 1 uneven end of the butted lace rectangle. If using conventional scissors, place a T-square ruler against the 2 sides of the lace rectangle. Draw a line across the width and cut.

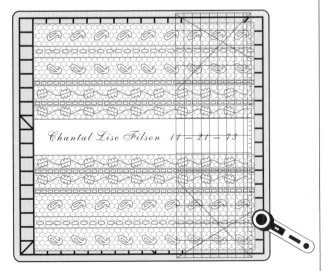

2. Measure the width of the butted lace piece. Using this measurement, cut a square from the butted lace.

3. Cut the ⅛"-wide (3mm) ribbon in half, forming two 9"-long (23cm) pieces. Weave a ribbon through each piece of lace beading. With a tapestry needle, weave the embroidery floss through the entre d'eux closest to the lace beading. *Do not cut the excess ribbon and floss tails yet!* Trim ⅛" (3mm) corners from the square.

Trim ⅛" (3mm)

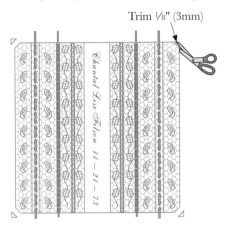

Finishing

1. Fold the batiste piece in half lengthwise and finger-press. Unfold. Repeat, folding in half on the crosswise grain. Unfold.

2. Cover the pinning board with a sheet of 8½" x 11" (21.5cm x 28cm) white paper. Place the batiste square on top of the paper. Place the lace square over the creased batiste, lining up the corners with the crease lines as shown below, so the lace square is on point in the batiste square.

3. Pin the lace to the batiste square. Staystitch (SL 1) ⅛" (3mm) from the outer edge of the lace. Zigzag (SW 2; SL .5) over the stitching. Trim away the excess floss and ribbon tails.

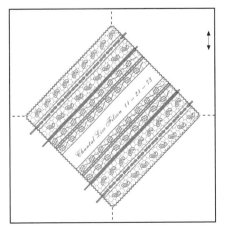

4. Trim away the batiste behind the lace square. From the back, spray-starch and press.

5. With a ruler and the Dixon pencil, mark the ribbon outline ⅛" (3mm) outside of the zigzag stitching. The ¼"-wide (6mm) ribbon will cover all edges and any unevenness of the lace square.

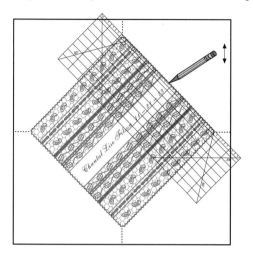

6. Allowing 5" (13cm) of ribbon to extend below the bottom corner of the batiste block, position the ¼"-wide (6mm) ribbon along the placement line drawn outside the lace square. Pin at the point of the square through the ribbon, batiste, and pinning board. Position the ribbon and pin. Use a dab of fabric glue stick to hold the ribbon in place for machine stitching as you position along the first side.

When you reach the corner, fold the ribbon as shown to create a 45° angle on the outside edge and a 90° angle on the inside edge. Make sure at this time that the ribbon covers all raw edges and machine stitching. Pin through the ribbon angle to hold it firmly. Consult the pattern.

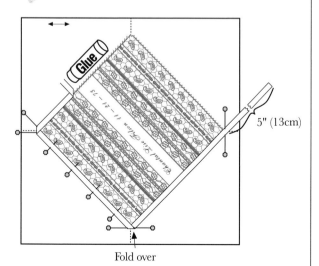

Fold over

7. Continue positioning and gluing the ribbon in the same manner around the remaining edges and corners. Wherever the ribbons cross, pin securely through all layers. Pin ribbon every ½" (1.25cm).

8. Edgestitch (SL 2) the outer edge of the ribbon in place. Use the edgestitching foot if you have one for your machine. Edgestitch the inner edge of the ribbon in place. Press work on the back. Make a bow in the ribbon after you have laundered the finished square. (See page 72.)

9. To tie a bow where the ribbons cross, bring the left tail over to the top, toward the center, forming a loop; pin. Repeat process on the other side. Unpin and repin. Refer to the pattern.

10. Bar-tack (SW 3; SL 0) the center of the bow. Cover the bar-tacking stitches with a button, lace rosette, or charm if desired.

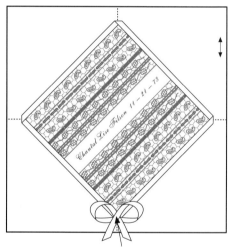

Bar-tack ribbon bow in place.

❧ THE HEIRLOOM QUILT ❧

The Heirloom Quilt, designed and sewn by Yolande Filson, 1993, Barrington, Illinois, 38" x 48".

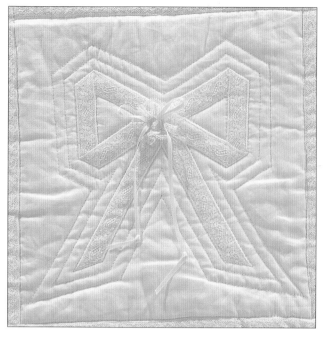

BOW

RAIL FENCE

HEART IN HAND

LOG CABIN

TRELLIS

ALL TIED UP

HEART

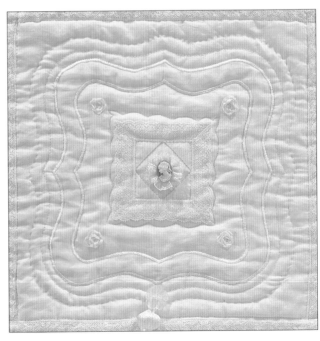

VICTORIAN ATTIC WINDOW

GRANDMOTHER'S FAN

PINWHEEL

CRAZY QUILT

BASKET OF POINTS

Turn-of-the-Century Lampshade Cover by Roberta Przybylski, 1993, Hawthorn Woods, Illinois, 18"x 18". This lamp cover is an adaptation of the Rail Fence design. The delicate web of threads in the French laces and Swiss embroidery soften the rays of light from the crystal lamp.

Grandmother's Table Topper, designed by Roberta Przybylski, 1993, Hawthorn Woods, Illinois, 20" x 20". Four Grandmother's Fan blocks are joined together with lace insertions to form a full circle design. Sewn by Karen Janis.

Grandmother's Fan Pillow by Yolande Filson, 1993, Barrington, Illinois, 16" x 16". This envelope pillow features the Grandmother's Fan design. The fan motif is outlined with lace edging and highlighted with pearl buttons.

Boudoir Box by Karen Janis, Karen Keepsakes, 1993, Chicago, Illinois, 8" x 8". This padded box has a lid covered with the Pinwheel design and is embellished with a lace rosette, button ribbons, and floss. It is an ideal place for jewelry as well as stationery.

The Light Catcher by Yolande Filson, 1993, Barrington, Illinois, 12" x 12". The liberal use of hemstitching enhances the Heart design and the border while letting the light shine through the open work. Assembled and sewn by Yolande Filson and Karen Janis.

Fantasy Bows by Roberta Przybylski, 1993, Hawthorn Woods, Illinois, 16" x 52". This table runner is an adaptation of the Trellis, Heart, and Bow design blocks. Assembled by Karen Janis.

Tic-tac-toe Board Game by Yolande Filson, 1993, Barrington, Illinois, 8" x 8". This adaptation of the Trellis block design uses lace edging and insertions to frame the game. The playing pieces are pearl buttons painted with miniature roses by Jolene Checchin, fabric artist, Chicago, Illinois.

ALL TIED UP

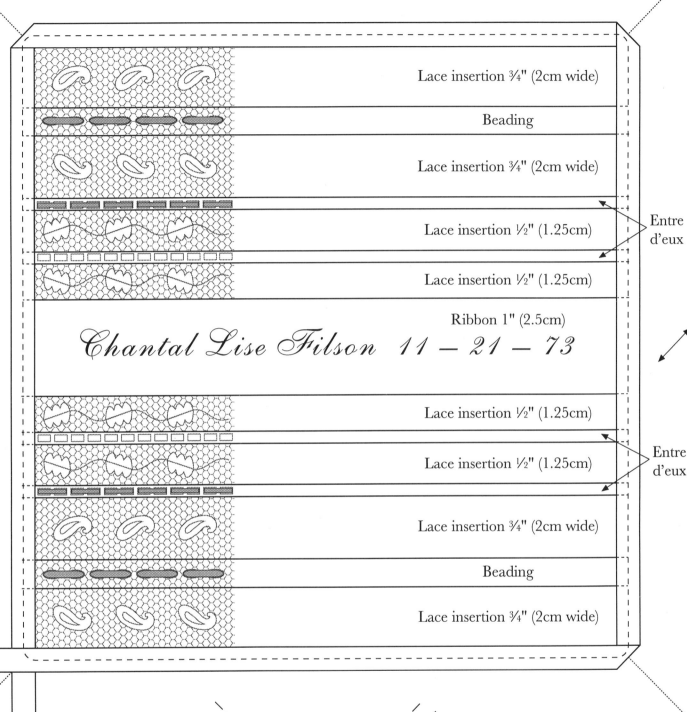

Lace insertion ¾" (2cm wide)

Beading

Lace insertion ¾" (2cm wide)

Lace insertion ½" (1.25cm)

Entre d'eux

Lace insertion ½" (1.25cm)

Ribbon 1" (2.5cm)

Chantal Lise Filson 11 — 21 — 73

Lace insertion ½" (1.25cm)

Lace insertion ½" (1.25cm)

Entre d'eux

Lace insertion ¾" (2cm wide)

Beading

Lace insertion ¾" (2cm wide)

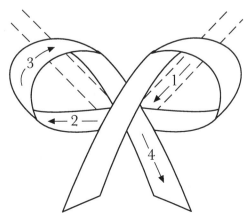

········· Creased line

░░░░ Lace placement

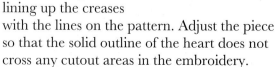 HEART

Hearts are a recurring theme in quilt patterns, new and old. Although the heart symbolizes love, friendship, and undying faithfulness, in times past it also carried another message. To include a heart in your quilt invited spinsterhood, so only brides or those betrothed used this motif in their handiwork. Today, hearts abound in quilt patterns and carry no such superstition.

"The heart has its reasons which reason knows not."
Blaise Pascal

Techniques
Circular Shaping
Lace Mitering an Outside Corner
Lace Mitering an Inside Corner

Materials
1 piece Swiss batiste, 11" square (28cm)
1 embroidered handkerchief (See step 3 in "Preparation" at right.)
⅝ yd. (57cm) of ⅝"-wide (1.5cm) lace insertion
#60/2 fine cotton thread
#60/8 sewing-machine needle
1 package flat-head pins (Clover)
Fine silk pins
Dixon washout chalk pencil
Open-toe or clear machine-embroidery foot
Optional: 2" (5cm) square of water-soluble stabilizer
Appliqué scissors

Spray starch
Pinning Board (See page 13.)

Preparation
Trace the pattern on page 49 onto a large sheet of white paper.

1. Mark the lengthwise grain line on the edge of the batiste square. Spray-starch and press the batiste and embroidered handkerchief section.
2. Fold the batiste in half lengthwise with the grain and finger-press. Unfold. Fold in half on the crosswise grain and finger-press. Unfold and set aside.
3. Cut a 6" (15cm) square from the corner of the embroidered handkerchief.
4. Place the embroidered hanky square right side up. Fold in half on the diagonal and finger-press to crease.
5. Place the heart pattern on the pinning board. Lay the embroidered piece on the pattern, lining up the creases with the lines on the pattern. Adjust the piece so that the solid outline of the heart does not cross any cutout areas in the embroidery.

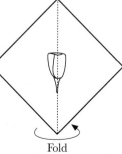

Fold

Note: If the heart does not show through the fabric, make a heart template to place on top for positioning purposes.

6. When pleased with the location of the embroidered design within the heart, pin through all layers (handkerchief, pattern, and pinning board) to stabilize the work. Then trace the heart outline onto the embroidered piece and mark the center with a dot. Unpin and remove the embroidered piece and the pattern.

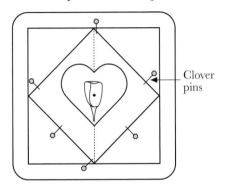

Clover pins

7. Place the batiste square on a smooth, hard surface. With the embroidered piece face up, put a pin through the center dot and then through the center of the batiste. Pin to the batiste so that the pins inside the marked heart will not interfere with the presser foot of the sewing machine.

Sewing

1. Staystitch (SL 2) on the marked line. Trim away the embroidered piece about ¼" (6mm) from the stitching line all the way around.

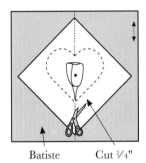

Batiste   Cut ¼"

2. Place the heart pattern on the pinning board again and lay the batiste square on top, lining up the heart with the outline on the sheet. Pin through all layers at the center and each corner. Mark the lace-insertion outline. Unpin and remove the pattern sheet.

Lace Mitering an Outside Corner

1. Fold the lace insertion in half crosswise and crease. Spray-starch only the center section, about 2" (5cm) on each side of the creased line, and steam-press the entire lace strip. *Spray only the center section* as the starch will make it difficult to shape the heart.

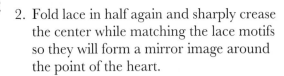

2. Fold lace in half again and sharply crease the center while matching the lace motifs so they will form a mirror image around the point of the heart.

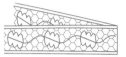

3. Use a pin to hold the lace layers together. Fold again just below the lace heading to form a 45° angle and finger-press on the diagonal from point AA to point BB to mark the sewing line for the miter. Remove the pin and unfold the lace.

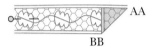

AA

BB

Fold to form 45° angle.

4. Place a small piece of water-soluble stabilizer on the throat plate of your machine under the presser foot. Hold the bobbin and top threads together as you begin to straight-stitch (SL 2) from point AA to point BB. Lift the presser foot, turn the lace over, and stitch on top of the first stitching.

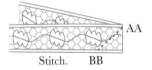

Stitch.   BB   AA

5. Unfold the stitched lace. The lace heading on the outside corner should be continuous.

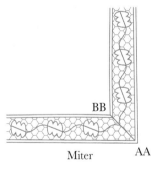

BB

Miter   AA

6. Place the lace on the point of the heart pattern to check for fit. The point should lie flat from A to B, and the lace should follow the heart outline (in the lower half of the heart only). Trim away the excess lace at the mitered point.

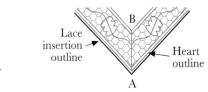

Lace insertion outline

Heart outline

A

B

Circular Shaping

1. Cover the pinning board with a sheet of white paper. Place the batiste square on top and pin through all the layers at each corner. Place the mitered lace over the heart point, right side up.

2. Using the flat-head pins, pin the mitered corner of the lace to points A and B on the batiste square. Continue pinning every inch or less on the lace headings until the heart begins to curve. Place the pins so the pinheads are as flat as possible, out of the way for pressing.

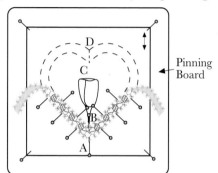

Pinning Board

3. Working along the outer edge of the lace on one side of the heart, place a pin every ¼" (6mm) or less, ending at the inner corner CD. Pin at D. Repeat on the remaining side of the heart.

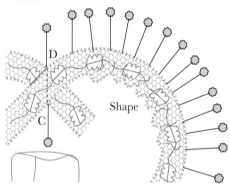

Shape

4. About ¼" (6mm) from the end of the lace tail, unravel the thread closest to the edge of the inner lace heading. (See "Lace Gathering" on page 11.) Gently pull the gathering thread and work the fullness evenly all the way around the curved area of the heart. Pin at C. Repeat on the other half of the heart. Unpin at D and repin through the 2 intersecting lace layers. Repeat at C. The lace ends will be crossed. At this point, check the shape of your heart and adjust as needed.

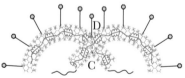

5. Steam the lace, then use your fingers to flatten and shape the lace. Use the point of a pin to help with the shaping. Allow to cool.

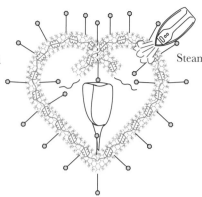

Steam

Lace Mitering an Inside Corner

1. Remove the pin at C, leaving the pin at D to stabilize the work. Fold under the top lace strip on top so that the 2 lace tails lie with one on top of the other. Pin in place at C. Mark the intersecting lines at C and D and unpin to remove the lace from the batiste square.

2. With right sides together, straight-stitch (SL 2) from D to C. Lift the presser foot, turn the lace over, and stitch on top of the first stitching from C to D. Trim away excess lace close to stitching.

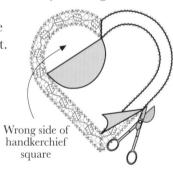

Fold

Miter

3. Return the lace heart to the batiste square. Pin in place with silk pins at points A, B, C, and D and then all around the heart outline. If you prefer, hand baste the heart-shaped lace insertion in place.

4. Removing the pins as you reach each one, staystitch (SL 2) in the outer lace heading first. Then staystitch the inside edge. Zigzag (SW 2; SL .5) over the staystitching.

5. Trim away the batiste behind the lace and the heart.

6. Place the completed piece face down on a towel-covered ironing board. Spray-starch and press from the back.

7. Reinforce the mitered seams on top with a zigzag or serpentine stitch (SW 2 and SL 1).

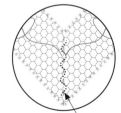

Wrong side of handkerchief square

Reinforce mitered seams at top and point with Serpentine Stitch.

Heart

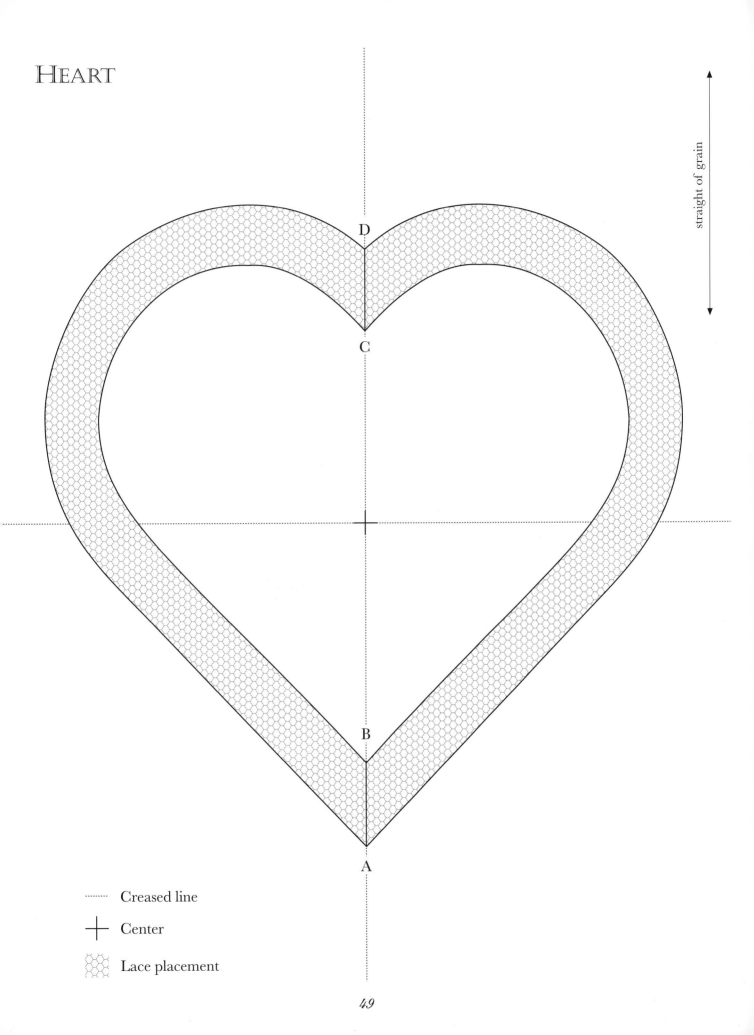

straight of grain

D

C

B

A

...... Creased line

＋ Center

▨ Lace placement

♠ ♠ VICTORIAN ATTIC WINDOW

*T*his block is our interpretation of an ornate window, linking our past ancestors to our present generation through heirloom quilting. We named it for a popular patchwork pattern, Attic Window. This pattern gained popularity around the 1940s. Before that, when women were living in a more rural setting, the pattern was called "Doves in the Window." It was then the custom to have a special window near the barn rafters for pet pigeons to enter or roost.

Techniques
Diamond Fold-Back
Cutwork Appliqué
Lace Mitering

Materials
1 piece of Swiss batiste, 11" (28cm) square
1 piece of cotton organdy, 11" (28cm) square
1 piece of cotton netting, 4" (10cm) square
½ yd. (46cm) of ¾"-wide (2cm) lace edging
11" (28cm) square of water-soluble stabilizer
#60/2 fine cotton thread
White rayon machine-embroidery thread
#60/8 sewing-machine needle
Spray starch
Dixon washout chalk pencil
Flat head and fine silk pins

Pinning Board (See page 13.)
See-through ruler
Open-toe or clear machine-embroidery foot
Appliqué scissors
Optional embellishments:
    Machine embroideries
    Bouillon roses (See page 65.)
    Cameo, buttons, lace appliqué, or small
       brooch for the center window

Preparation
Trace the pattern on page 53 onto a large sheet of white paper.
1. Mark the grainline on the edge of the batiste, organdy, and netting squares. Spray-starch and press the squares and the lace edging.
2. Fold each fabric square in half lengthwise and finger-press the crease. Unfold each one, then fold each in half crosswise and finger-press to crease. Unfold and mark the center on each one with a dot. Set aside.
3. Place the pattern on the pinning board.
4. Place a pin through the center dot on the netting and pin to the center of the pattern. Adjust so the creases match the lines on the pattern. Pin netting to the pinning board at all 4 corners.

5. Trace the center-square outline onto the netting. The small see-through ruler comes in handy here. Remove the pins.

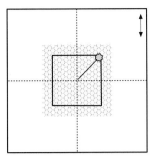

6. Center the netting over the batiste square and pin in position, placing pins away from the stitching line.

Sewing

1. With the cotton thread in both the bobbin and needle, straight-stitch (SL 1.5) over the marked lines on the netting. Remove the pins.

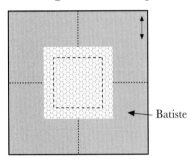

Batiste

2. Measure to make sure that the creased lines on the batiste form 4 equal squares. Draw new lines if necessary and ignore the creased lines.

3. Turn the batiste square over and carefully *cut the batiste only* on the creased lines inside the stitching that outlines the inner square. *Do not cut the netting.*

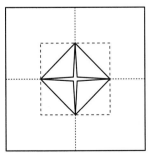

Cut batiste on creased lines.

4. Turn back the resulting points, creating a diagonal fold on each one and exposing the netting. Finger-press each fold.

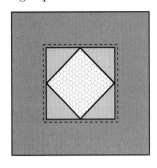

5. Unfold the points and straight-stitch next to the crease line (toward the outer corners of the stitched square) as shown.

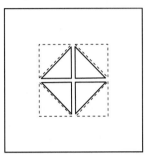

6. Fold the points back to cover the stitching and pin in place. Zigzag (SW 1; SL 1) over the raw edges.

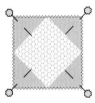

7. Place the pattern over the pinning board and center the net/batiste design on top. Pin.

8. Miter lace edging around the center square as shown for the Trellis block, beginning on page 30. Position the lace heading on top of the zigzag stitching around the outer edge of the center square created in the previous steps.

9. After completing the mitering and stitching (SL 2) the lace in place, turn the work over and trim away excess netting. Press if needed.

10. Zigzag or serpentine-stitch (SW 1; SL 1) over the mitered lace corners and along the outer scalloped lace edge.

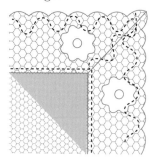

11. Place the pattern sheet on the pinning board. Put the batiste square on top with the design centered. Pin through all layers at each outer corner of the batiste square. Trace both curved design lines onto the batiste. Unpin.

12. Place the organdy square on top of the square of water-soluble stabilizer. Place the batiste square on top with grainlines matching. Pin the layers together, working from the center out and keeping pins away from the marked design lines.

13. With white rayon embroidery thread in the needle and in the bobbin, satin-stitch (SW 1.5; SL 2.5) around the center square, covering the lace heading with stitching.

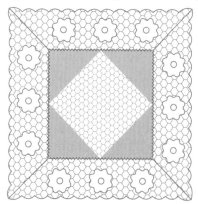

14. Leaving the machine threaded with rayon thread, zigzag (SW 1; SL 1) over the curved lines. Pivot on the inside needle swing for the inside corners and on the outside needle swing for the outside corners.

15. Staystitch ¼" (6mm) from the outer edges of the block. This keeps all layers together to prevent shifting. Unpin and trim away the batiste inside the curvy lines to expose the organdy.

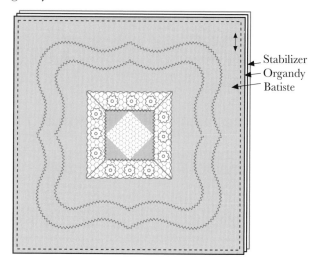

Stabilizer
Organdy
Batiste

16. Satin-stitch (SW 2; SL .25) over the inside and then the outside curvy design lines. The stitching should cover all the previous stitching as well as the raw edges.

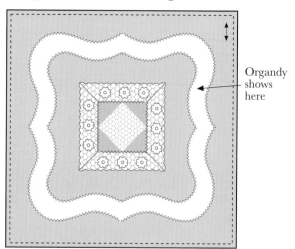

Organdy shows here

17. Trim away as much of the stabilizer as possible. Any remaining stabilizer will dissolve when the block is laundered. See page 72.

18. Make a lace rosette for the center of the block, referring to the directions on page 18. Hand stitch in place and sew a cameo, button, rose, or small brooch in the center.

VICTORIAN ATTIC WINDOW

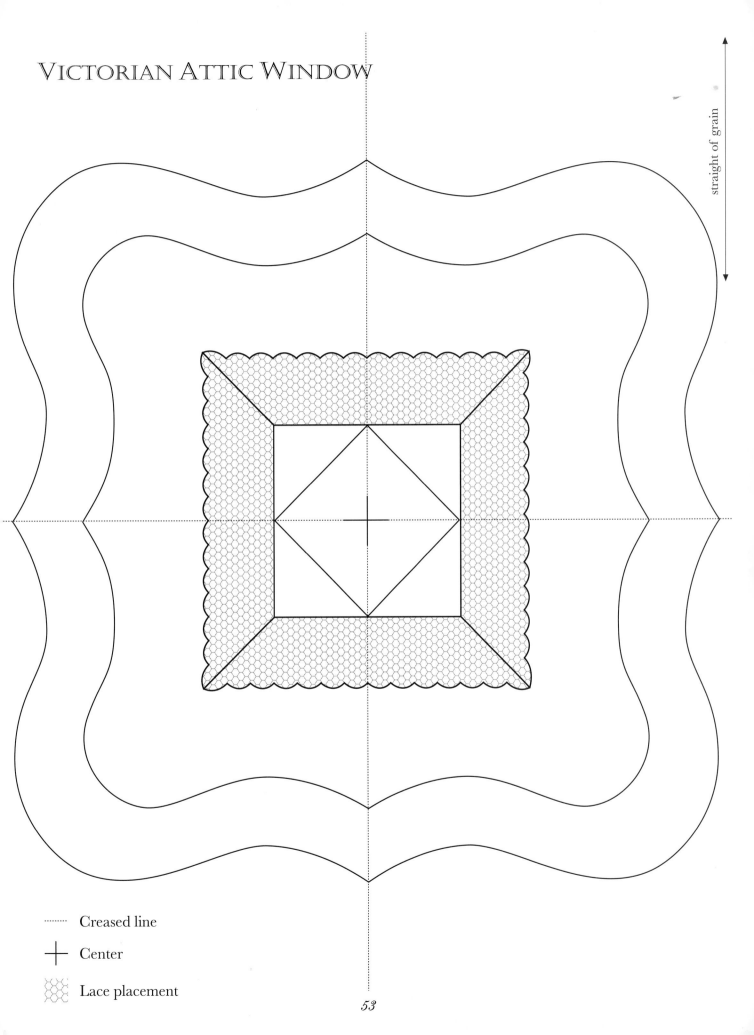

straight of grain

...... Creased line

+ Center

Lace placement

🌸🌸 GRANDMOTHER'S FAN

After the 1876 Centennial Exhibition in Philadelphia, the fan became a very popular quilting design with American women. This was due in part to the Japanese artists who featured the fan motif in their fine hand embroideries. Different versions include the Imperial Fan, the Friendship Fan, and Fanny's Fan, but none were as popular as Grandmother's Fan.

Techniques

Hemstitching
Lace Shaping
Ribbon Shaping
Puffing
Lace-Motif Application

Materials

1 piece Swiss batiste, 11" (28cm) square
1 piece Swiss batiste, 2½" x 44" (6cm x 112cm)
    cut on the true cross grain of the fabric
    (See "Pulling a Thread" on page 10.)
½ yd. (46cm) of ½"-wide (1.25cm) lace insertion
½ yd. (46cm) of 1¼"- or 1½"-wide (3cm to 4cm)
    lace edging with beading along the
    straight edge
⅜ yd. (34cm) of ¼"-wide (6mm) ribbon
1 piece of water-soluble stabilizer, 12" (31cm)
    square
Lace motif, fan corner, or a small section of
    textured fabric, at least 4" x 4" (19cm x 19cm)
Quilting thread

#60/2 fine cotton thread
#60/8 sewing-machine needle
#100/16 wing needle
Optional: gathering foot
Optional: edgestitching foot
Open-toe or clear machine-embroidery foot
Spray starch
Dixon washout chalk pencil
1 skein embroidery floss
Tapestry needle
Flat-head and fine silk pins
Pinning Board (See page 13.)
Appliqué scissors

Preparation

Use the pattern on the pullout pattern sheet.

1. Mark the grain line on the edge of the batiste square. Spray-starch, press, and iron the batiste square and the lace insertion on both sides.
2. Place the pattern on the pinning board. Lay the 11" (28cm) square of batiste over the fan design, making sure to match the grain-line directions on the fabric and the pattern. Pin through all layers (batiste, pattern, and pinning board) at each corner to stabilize.
3. Trace all the solid and dotted lines of the fan design Lines 1, 2, 3, A, B, C, and the spokes.
4. Unpin and place the marked batiste square over the square of water-soluble stabilizer. Pin the layers together.

5. Center lace insertion over 1 fan spoke. (Refer to the pattern.) Pin the lace to the batiste and cut away the excess lace, allowing ¼" (6mm) of lace to extend beyond the curved stitching lines (A and B). Position, pin, and trim lace for the remaining spokes, matching the lace-design motif to the motifs in the first spoke.

6. Put a #60/8 needle in the machine. With #60/2 cotton thread on the top and in the bobbin, staystitch (SL 2.5) in the lace heading on both sides of each lace strip. Always stitch in the same direction on each strip to prevent puckering.

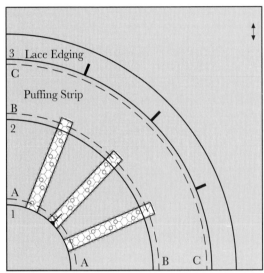

Hemstitching

This technique is also called pin stitching or entre d'eux stitching.

1. Practice on a separate piece of fabric before stitching on your batiste square. Place a #100/16 wing needle in your machine and thread the needle and bobbin with cotton thread.

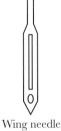

Wing needle

2. Consult your sewing-machine instruction manual for the correct setting on your machine for hemstitching. The normal recommendation is 2 to 2.5 for both the stitch width and length.

A regular hemstitch has one swing of the needle in the lace heading and the other swing of the needle in the batiste to create the look of entre d'eux.

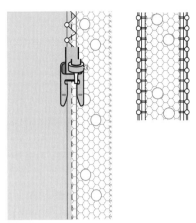

If your machine is not equipped with a hemstitch, zigzag (SW 2.5; SL 1.5) for a similar effect.

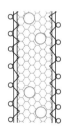

3. After practicing on scraps, hemstitch along each edge of the lace spokes.

Lace Shaping

1. At each end of the lace edging, pull the thread that is closest to the straight edge (heading) to gather it. (See "Gathering Lace" on page 11.)

2. Place the gathered lace over the lace-edging outline on the pattern design sheet and adjust the gathers to fit. Transfer the shaped lace to the ironing board and steam-press. This will not be an exact fit at this point. Spray-starch and press. Allow to cool in place before handling.

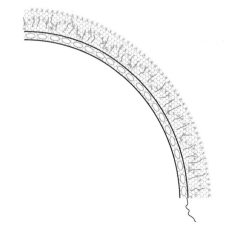

Ribbon Shaping

1. Soak the ribbon in clear water, then squeeze out the water through your fingers.
2. Place the ribbon over a towel-covered ironing board. Pin 1 end of the ribbon to the ironing board. With the iron set at a temperature as high as the ribbon can withstand, slowly iron the ribbon while shaping it into a curve with the other hand. This is easier than it sounds. Repeat the procedure until the ribbon has the curved shape outlined on the pattern sheet. Allow to cool.

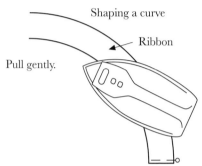

Shaping a curve

Ribbon

Pull gently.

Puffing

1. Replace wing needle with a #60/8 sewing-machine needle. Steam-press the batiste strip that was cut on the true cross grain. Fold the strip in half crosswise and finger-press to crease the fold. Fold in half again into quarters and finger-press the folds to crease.
2. Unfold the strip and use a pencil to mark the creases only within the top and bottom ¼" (6mm) of the strip.

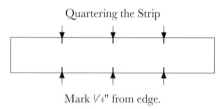

Quartering the Strip

Mark ¼" from edge.

3. Fill a bobbin with quilting thread. (Quilting thread is coated and stronger than regular cotton thread, making it ideal for gathering.) Place the gathering foot on the machine. (See the note following step 4.)
4. Hold the top and bottom threads together for the first 2 to 3 stitches and *slowly* stitch (SL 3) ¼" (6mm) from each long edge of the batiste strip. Keep the edge of the presser foot parallel to the edge of the batiste. As you stitch, the gathering foot will cause the fabric to gather.

Note: If a gathering foot is not available, straight-stitch (SL 2.5) ¼" (6mm) from the raw edge and pull on the quilting thread in the bobbin to gather.

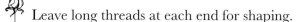

Leave long threads at each end for shaping.

5. Place the pattern on the pinning board. Place the batiste square with hemstitched fan spokes on top of the pattern. Pin at each outer corner to stabilize.
6. Line up the bottom edge of the puffing strip with the solid line #2. Match the markings on the outer curve of the puffing strip to the spoke lines and pin.
7. Pin on the bottom edge of the puffing strip, placing a pin where the center spoke and the center marking on the puffing strip meet. Pin at the remaining spokes in the same manner.
8. Adjust the fullness by pulling on the quilting thread and redistributing the gathers or by holding the quilting thread and spreading the shirred fabric. After the required shape has been achieved, check to see that the gathers are radiating from the center out in a straight line. If necessary, use the point of a pin to adjust the gathers. See illustration below.
9. Place additional pins along the inner and outer curved edges, making sure that the puffing strip begins and ends at the outer edges of the batiste square.
10. Holding the iron about ¼" (6mm) above the puffing strip, apply steam. *The iron should not touch the fabric;* you have a water-soluble stabilizer underneath your work that you do not want to dissolve and you do not want to flatten the gathers in the puffing strip. Allow to cool.
11. Replace the quilting thread in the bobbin with #60/2 thread.
12. Remove the batiste square from the pinning board and straight-stitch (SL 2.5) the puffing strip to the batiste on top of the gathering stitches along the inner and outer curved edges.
13. Trim the puffing strip ⅛" (3mm) from the stitching on the outer and inner edges. This eliminates excess bulk.

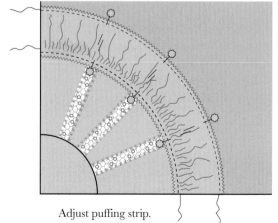

Adjust puffing strip.

Ribbon Application

1. Pin the shaped ribbon in place over the inner curved edge of the puffing strip to cover the raw edges.
2. Edgestitch (SL 2–2.5) ribbon in place along the top edge first (Line B) and then along the lower edge (Line 2). Don't worry if Line 2 is not completely covered with the ribbon. The line will disappear in the washing. (See page 72.)

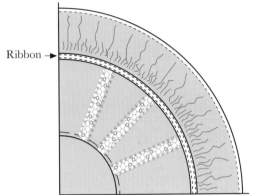

Ribbon →

Lace-Edging Application

1. Pin the gathered lace edging over the curved outer edge of the puffing strip (Line C). Staystitch (SL 2) in the lace heading on the inside curve.
2. Stitch (SL 2) the remaining edge of the lace in place, following the scalloped shaping.
3. Zigzag (SW 1.5; SL 1) in the lace heading and along the scalloped edge.

Finishing

Choose Method I when using a lace motif for the fan corner and Method II when using fabric.

Method I

1. Pin the lace motif right side up over the corner section of the fan.
2. Zigzag (SW 1.5; SL 1) in place to cover the spoke ends.

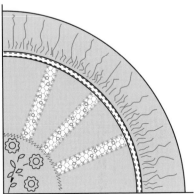

3. Cut away the water-soluble stabilizer. Any stabilizer that remains will dissolve when you wash the quilt. (See page 72.)
4. Using appliqué scissors, trim away the batiste behind the spokes of the lace edging. From the front, press over all your work, except the puffing.
5. With a tapestry needle, weave 6 strands of embroidery floss through the beading on the lace edging.

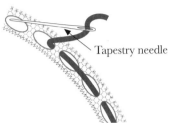

Tapestry needle

Method II

Note: If a corner motif is not available, use a piece of textured cotton jacquard or pique to cover the spoke ends, following the directions below.

1. Make a template for the corner piece on the pullout pattern. Place the template on the fabric and trace around it, marking the center.
2. On the batiste square, trim away the lower corner by cutting on Line 1.
3. With right sides together, pin the corner piece to the fan, matching centers and clipping the lower edge of the fan if necessary for a smooth fit. Stitch (SL 2) ¼" (6mm) from the raw edges.

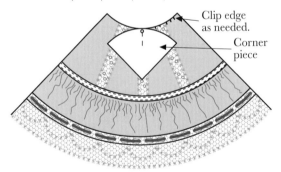

Clip edge as needed.

Corner piece

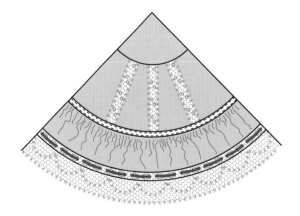

✿ ✿ Pinwheel

The Pinwheel pattern is a popular traditional patchwork pattern. It is also called "Flutter Wheel" and "Fly Wheel." The wheel played a significant part in the daily life of pioneer women and was essential for survival in both a spiritual and economic sense. Women's quilt designs were a reflection of daily observances. The Pinwheel design reflected the constant forward movement of the slow-moving wagons heading west and the blowing winds that powered the windmills to produce water.

Techniques

*Butting Lace Insertion to Lace Beading
Butting Swiss Entre d'eux to Lace Insertion
Diagonal Sewing*

Materials

1 piece of Swiss batiste, about 6" x 27"
   (15cm x 69cm)
2 yds. (182cm) of ⅝"-wide (1.5cm) French lace insertion
1 yd. (91cm) of ⅜"-wide (9mm) lace beading
1¼ yds. (114cm) of ⅛"-wide (3mm) ribbon
½ yd. (46cm) of ⅝"-wide (1.5cm) Swiss insertion with entre d'eux edges
#60/2 fine cotton thread
#100/3 sewing thread
#60/8 sewing-machine needle
Dixon washout chalk pencil
Spray starch

Rotary cutter, ruler, and mat
Open-toe or clear machine-embroidery foot
Edgestitching foot, blind hem foot, or any presser foot designed with a separating guide
Optional: 2" (5cm) square of water-soluble stabilizer

Preparation

Refer to the pattern on page 62.

1. Spray-starch, press, and iron laces and batiste.
2. Fold the French lace insertion in half crosswise and cut along the fold so you have 2 pieces of the same length.

Sewing

1. Thread the sewing machine with fine cotton thread in the needle and on the bobbin. Attach the edgestitching foot with a separating bar to help keep the lace strips from overlapping while you stitch.
2. Place the lace beading next to a strip of French lace insertion and position under the needle with a small piece of water-soluble stabilizer underneath. Hold the top and bottom threads together and zigzag (SW 1.5 to 2; SL 1) the lace edges together. This is called "butting." See the illustration at the top of page 59.

3. Steam-press the resulting lace strip to remove any distortion that might have occurred during the sewing process. If necessary, starch again and allow to cool.

4. Lay the remaining piece of the French insertion strip along the remaining edge of the lace beading and butt as described above, lining up the lace motifs so they form a mirror image with those in the first strip of insertion if possible. Spray-starch, press, and iron the completed strip.

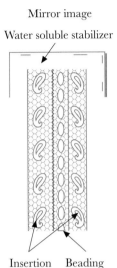

Mirror image

Water soluble stabilizer

Insertion   Beading

5. Fold the assembled lace strip in half crosswise and cut along the fold. Set the 2 resulting pieces aside.

6. Trim away the batiste seam allowance on each side of the entre d'eux edge on the Swiss insertion strip.

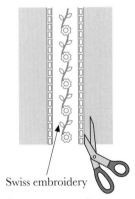

Swiss embroidery

Cut away seam allowances.

7. Place the trimmed Swiss insertion right side up next to an assembled strip and butt with zigzag stitching. Steam-press to remove any distortion that might have occurred during the sewing process. Allow to cool.

8. Butt and stitch the remaining lace strip to the other edge of the Swiss entre d'eux. The completed piece should look like the illustration at top right. Spray-starch, press, iron, and allow to cool before handling.

9. Place a ruler along one edge of the completed lace strip to make sure it is straight. To remove any distortion, steam and spray-starch the

assembled strip. Then press and line up the outside lace edge with the straight edge of a pressing cloth or fabric square. Block gently to straighten.

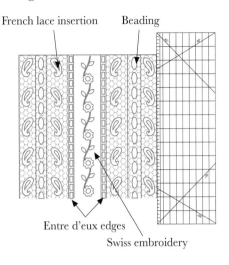

French lace insertion   Beading

Entre d'eux edges

Swiss embroidery

Cutting

1. Measure the width of the assembled lace strip. It should be approximately 3¼" wide (8.2cm). It might be slightly narrower or wider, depending on your machine and the stitch width used in the butting process.

2. Using the width you determined in step 1, cut 4 identical squares from the assembled lace strip. Lay the squares next to each other with the lace running in the same direction. Weave ribbon through the beading in each square, leaving a ½"-long (1.25cm) tail at each end.

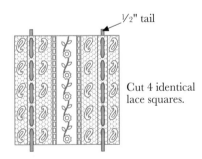

½" tail

Cut 4 identical lace squares.

3. Cut 4 batiste squares, each the same size as the lace squares and mark the lengthwise grain on each.

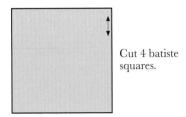

Cut 4 batiste squares.

4. With a newly sharpened pencil, draw a diagonal line from one corner across to the opposite corner on each batiste square.

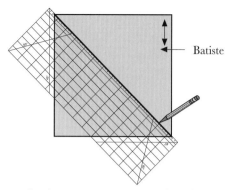

Batiste

5. Place a batiste square on top of each lace square, with the diagonal line pointing in the same direction on each one. Pin across the line.

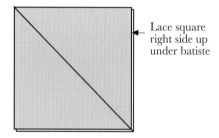

Lace square right side up under batiste

Sewing

1. Replace the regular presser foot with the embroidery foot. With regular sewing thread on the machine and using a straight stitch (SL 1.5), sew just to the left of the diagonal line, about 1/16" (2mm) away, on each batiste square.

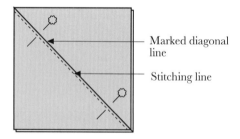

Marked diagonal line

Stitching line

2. Turn the batiste square down over the stitched line so that the raw edges are even on the adjacent sides of the batiste triangle

that forms; finger-press. You will treat the 2 layers of batiste in each pinwheel square as 1 layer during the sewing process.

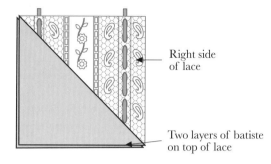

Right side of lace

Two layers of batiste on top of lace

3. On the wrong side of each square, cut away the lace triangle behind the double layer of the batiste, leaving a 1/8"-wide (3mm) seam allowance. Be careful not to cut into the batiste. Spray-starch, press, and iron all the square sections.

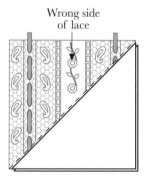

Wrong side of lace

4. Lay out all the squares as shown below. Sew the blocks together in pairs with right sides together and using a 1/8"-wide (3mm) seam. Stitch with the lace on top and trim excess ribbon even with the edge of the seam. Press the seams toward the batiste.

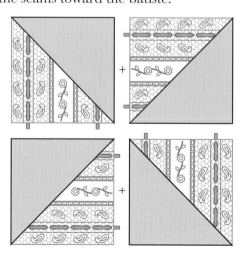

5. Pin and sew the pairs together to complete the center Pinwheel block. Press the resulting seam flat, then open out the pinwheel and press with the seam toward the batiste, making sure the lace seams are hidden.

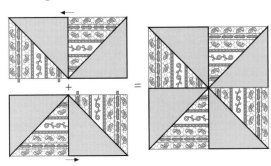

6. From the remainder of the batiste strip, cut 2 pieces, each 6" (15.2cm) square. Cut each square once diagonally, forming 4 identical triangles.

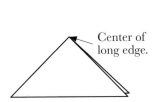

7. Fold each triangle in half along the longest edge to locate the center and finger-press to crease.

Center of long edge.

8. Pin a batiste triangle to one side of the pinwheel with right sides together, matching the center crease on the batiste triangle with the center seam of the pinwheel. Approximately 1" (2.5cm) of batiste will extend beyond the edges of the pinwheel.

With the batiste triangle on the top, use a straight stitch (SL 1.5) to sew the 2 layers together. Begin stitching from the edge of the pinwheel triangle point and use a ⅛"-wide (3mm) seam allowance. End the stitching 1½" (3.7cm) from the bottom of the triangle point.

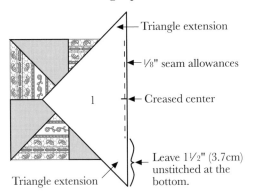

Triangle extension

⅛" seam allowances

Creased center

1

Leave 1½" (3.7cm) unstitched at the bottom.

Triangle extension

Note: The opening left at the end of this seam will be closed after adding the fourth batiste triangle to the pinwheel. This technique gives the illusion that the pinwheel is in motion. Finger-press the seam toward the batiste triangle.

9. With right side up, rotate pinwheel in a clockwise fashion. Add the next triangle, matching the centers as before. Stitch with the batiste triangle on the top. After stitching, trim the excess batiste on triangle #1. Finger-press the seam as you did for triangle #1.

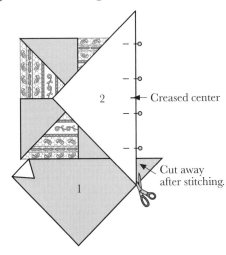

2

Creased center

1

Cut away after stitching.

10. Add triangle #3 in the same manner and trim.

11. To add triangle #4, fold back and pin the point on triangle #1 to keep it out of the way of the stitching. Pin triangle #4 in place and use a straight stitch to sew the seam as for the other triangles.

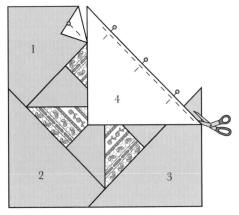

1

4

2

3

Stitch from Pinwheel side.

12. Complete the seam joining triangle #1 to the pinwheel and triangle #4. Unpin triangle point #1 and place on top of triangle #4 with right sides together. Use a straight stitch for the remaining 1½" (3.8cm). Finger-press the seam, then spray-starch, press, and iron the completed block.

PINWHEEL

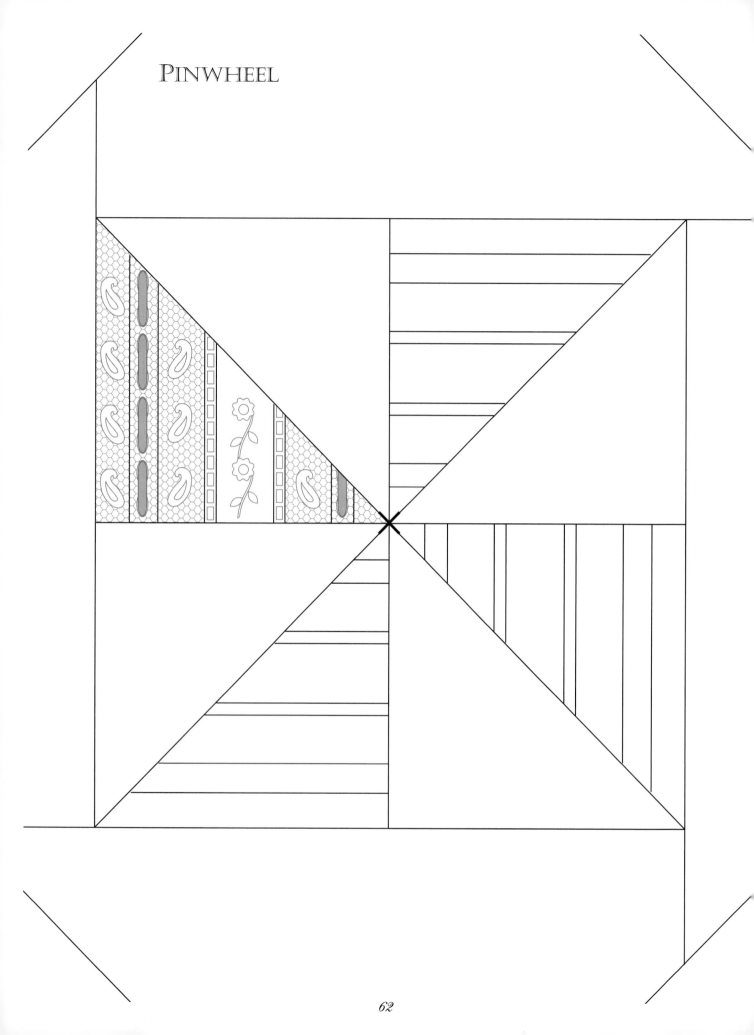

CRAZY QUILT

razy quilts are the fabric of life. During the Victorian era, this type of unstructured piecing provided a creative outlet for women and was a reflection of life around them. A man's status in society reflected the quantity of free time his wife had for needlework. Bits and pieces of various fabrics, trimmings, and memorabilia were incorporated into a Victorian woman's quilt, and elaborate embroidery stitches exhibited her artistic abilities.

Unlike other blocks where precise cutting and sewing are of utmost importance, the Crazy Quilt block is usually assembled in a haphazard manner. The random pieced sections add interest and allow you much creative freedom. We have provided a pattern sheet for this block, but if you are familiar with piecing on a foundation, you can certainly create your own design without the pattern.

If you have been hoarding laces, white fabric remnants, ribbons, handkerchiefs, doilies, snippets from other blocks, trinkets, and buttons, this is the place to use these special treasures and any leftover laces from the other completed squares. Before starting, wash carefully, towel dry, and press any antique laces you are going to incorporate into the block to make sure you are happy with the color. They may not turn out to be as white as you would like. A small scrap from your wedding dress and veil would make a meaningful memento to include in this block. Look upon this square as a life collage.

Techniques
Prairie Points
Crazy Quilt Piecing—Log Cabin Style
Embroidery Stitches:
Buttonhole Stitch
Cretan Stitch
Feather Stitch
French Knot

Materials
1 piece of organdy, 11" (28cm) square
Assorted scraps of a variety of white fabrics with texture and/or surface sheen, such as satin, jacquard, polished cotton pique, embroidered handkerchief, or napkin
Lace scraps left over from other blocks, crochet doilies, or any other precious snippets
Ribbons in assorted widths
Buttons and charms in various sizes
#60/3 rayon thread for piecing and machine embroidery
#60/8 sewing-machine needle
Cotton embroidery floss (DMC) for hand embroidery
Pinning Board (See page 13.)
Appliqué scissors
Open-toe or clear machine-embroidery foot

Preparation

Use the pattern on the pullout pattern sheet.

1. Make 3–5 Prairie Points for this block, using 1 of the 3 methods in the box at right.
2. Press and iron the organdy. It is the base fabric for the Crazy Quilt piecing. Mark the grain line.
3. Place the pattern on the pinning board. Place the organdy on top of the pattern and trace around the center section. Leave this area uncovered for an airy look at the center of the block.
4. Arrange fabric pieces around the marked center to determine the location for each piece and come up with a pleasing layout of the block components. Do not cut the pieces to match the shapes on the pattern; do not place heavy, textured fabrics in the outer areas; and work for a balanced look.

Piecing

1. When you are pleased with the design, carefully remove the organdy foundation piece without disturbing the design you have created.
2. Place the first piece right side down on the marked center and stitch ¼" (6mm) from the raw edges, extending the stitching past the marked lines on the organdy.

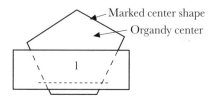

Marked center shape
Organdy center

3. Fold piece #1 back onto the organdy and press.

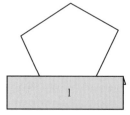

4. Rotate your work clockwise or counterclockwise; it depends on which way feels more comfortable to you. Lay the second fabric scrap on the next marked line with right sides together and raw edges even; stitch ¼" (6mm) from the raw edges. Make sure the stitching will cover the first piece of fabric when turned back onto the organdy. If necessary, trim away the excess fabric from the seam allowance. Fold back and press the second piece.

Prairie Points

Method I

1. Cut fabric squares, each 2" x 2" (5cm x 5cm). Working with 1 square at a time, fold in half on the diagonal.
2. Fold again to make a 4-layer triangle. Press.

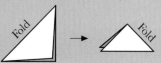

3. Insert the folded edge from 1 Prairie Point into the open edge of another. Pin and stitch together in a row ⅛" (3mm) from the raw edge.

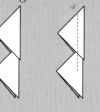

Method II

1. Cut fabric squares, each 2" x 2" (5cm x 5cm). Fold in half crosswise and finger-press.
2. Fold each end in to meet in the center. Press and stitch ⅛" (3mm) from the raw edges.

3. Arrange the finished points so that they line up point to point or overlap each other slightly as shown in the diagram.

Method III

1. For each Prairie Point, cut a 2"-long (5cm) piece of 1"-wide (2.5cm) ribbon. Fold in half, creasing slightly to mark the center.
2. Fold the 2 ends on the diagonal so the cut ends meet the bottom edge of the ribbon. Press. Pin and stitch ⅛" (3mm) from the raw edge.

Note: The Prairie Points made with Methods II and III have no right or wrong side. Use whichever side you like best.

Continue adding pieces until the foundation is covered, catching the prepared Prairie Points in one of the seams. You may also include pieces of lace in the seams for an overlaid appearance. Refer to the photo on page 63.

5. Eliminate bulk by cutting away any unnecessary fabric.

Embroidery Stitches

Add hand-embroidered details to as many of the seams as you wish. Hand embroidery adds a new dimension and a richness to your work. Use cotton embroidery floss, perle cotton, or silk ribbon. You may substitute machine-embroidery stitches for hand embroidery if you prefer. The machine feather stitch can be quite effective with rayon or other decorative thread over the seam.

If you would like to add lace appliqués to the completed block, satin-stitch (SW 1.5; SL 1) around the edges and trim away the fabric behind it. This will allow the second layer of quilt lining to show through.

Other Embellishments

Personalize your square with any of the following:

1. Bar-tack narrow ribbons to your block. Tie them into bows as decorative effects or tie them to great-grandmother's ring, baby's rattle or first pacifier, a lock of hair, or a ribbon from the baby bonnet. The possibilities are as endless as the memorabilia available to you.

2. When attaching a lace motif to your Crazy Quilt square, leave a small section open at the top to create a pocket for baby's first lost tooth.

3. Add buttons, laces, and ribbon rosettes (page 69) for decorative touches.

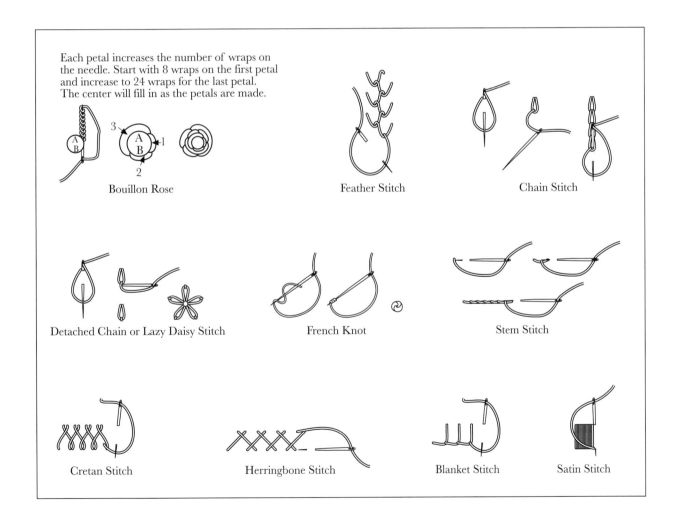

Each petal increases the number of wraps on the needle. Start with 8 wraps on the first petal and increase to 24 wraps for the last petal. The center will fill in as the petals are made.

Bouillon Rose

Feather Stitch

Chain Stitch

Detached Chain or Lazy Daisy Stitch

French Knot

Stem Stitch

Cretan Stitch

Herringbone Stitch

Blanket Stitch

Satin Stitch

🔔🔔🔔 BASKET OF POINTS

*T*he basket design symbolizes happiness and prosperity and was a favorite pattern for wedding quilts. The variations for both pieced and appliquéd Basket blocks are endless. This is an additional interpretation and one that particularly resembles the "Cherry Basket." The basket is an interpretation of Shark's Teeth, Prairie Points, and Sawtooth Edge, popular fabric-manipulation techniques borrowed from traditional quiltmaking.

These techniques have also been used to make ribbon ornaments for a lady's hat, as the finishing edge on antique quilts, or as a fashion detail on smocked dresses. As a young girl, I remember seeing white cotton organdy aprons and pinafores trimmed with rows of points on the pocket, bib, and hem edge. A small bouillon rose or lazy daisy stitches at the tip of the points added an embroidered touch, while keeping the points in place.

Techniques
Fold, Clip, and Point
Circular Shaping
Crisscross Running Stitch
Couching
French Knot Stitch
Ribbon Rosette

Materials
1 piece of Swiss batiste, 11"x 20" (28cm x 51cm)*
⅝ yd. (57cm) of ¼"-wide (6mm) satin or
    grosgrain ribbon
1 skein cotton embroidery floss

#10 crewel needle
Heavy spray starch
Dixon washout chalk pencil
See-through ruler
#60/8 sewing-machine needle
Fine silk pins
#60/2 fine cotton thread
Pinning Board (See page 13.)
Optional: even-feed foot (preferably equipped
    with a quilting guide)
Optional: rotary cutting mat with 1" grid
Masking tape

*Be sure to cut this piece with the longest side of the rectangle along the lengthwise grain. To be sure the rectangle is on grain, pull a thread on each edge. See page 10.

Preparation
Use the pattern on the pullout pattern sheet.
1. Place the Basket of Points pattern on your work table in full view.
2. Mark the lengthwise grain line on the edge of the fabric.
3. Fold the batiste in half and make sure that the edges meet exactly. If they lie off grain, pull gently on the diagonal to realign the grain lines.

4. Spray-starch and press batiste on both sides to give it a crisp finish.

5. Place the batiste rectangle on the grid of the rotary-cutting mat and use masking tape to secure. Make sure the fabric is lying on grain, using the grid lines as a guide.

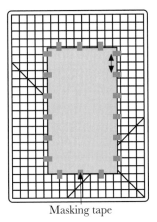

Masking tape

6. Using a pencil with a fine point, draw a line 1½" (4cm) from and parallel to the bottom edge of the batiste. Draw this line from left to right.

7. Draw the next line from right to left 1" (2.5cm) above the first. Draw 11 more parallel lines spaced 1" (2.5cm) apart, *alternating the direction you draw to avoid dragging and distorting the batiste.* Remove the tape.

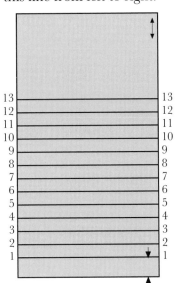

1 ½" (4cm)

8. Beginning at the bottom line, number each line at each end ¼" (6mm) in from the edge of the batiste. You should have 13 lines, beginning with line 1 at the bottom.

9. Make ⅛"-deep (3mm) clips on each end of each line.

10. Fold batiste on line 2, bringing lines 1 and 3 together to make the bottom tuck. Be sure to match clips at the outer edges. Pin lines 1 and 3 together, placing pins parallel with and through the marked lines. Crease line 2 by finger-pressing. Because you starched the fabric, it should take a sharp edge when finger-pressed. See the illustration with step 1 under "Sewing" at right.

Now take the time to make sure that the first fold is straight and lines 1 and 3 match exactly. If they do not, unpin and start again. If the first folded tuck is incorrect, it will get worse as you make the next tucks.

Tip: If you are unsure of how to proceed for this folding technique, practice first on an 11" x 20" (28cm x 51cm) piece of paper.

Sewing

An even-feed foot equipped with a quilting guide is very helpful for this block. If an even-feed foot is unavailable for your machine, consult your machine manual for other seam-guide options. There may be a quilting guide that slides into your regular presser foot in your machine accessory kit.

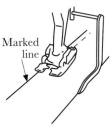

Even-feed foot

Marked line

Use a seam gauge to measure the width of the tuck and transfer that measurement to match the distance between the needle and the inside quilting arm.

1. With the fold positioned to your right under the presser foot, stitch 1 thread to the right of line 1.

Front

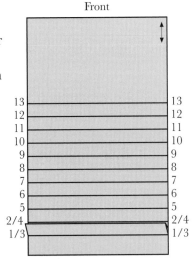

2. On the right side, turn the tuck toward the top of the batiste and finger-press to crease along the seam line. Line 2 should meet line 4.

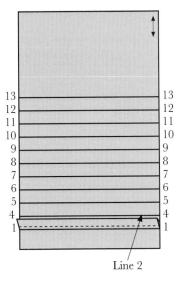

Line 2

3. Make the next tuck *on the right side of the work* by folding on line 6 to bring lines 5 and 7 together. Match the clipped edges and pin the lines together as you did to prepare the first tuck for stitching.

4. Stitch the tuck 1 thread to the right of line 5.

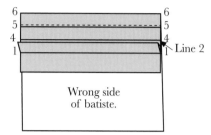

5. Turn the second tuck toward the bottom edge of the batiste and finger-press along the stitching line on the wrong side as you did the first tuck. The two folded edges of the stitched tucks should meet on the front. Don't worry if they overlap slightly.

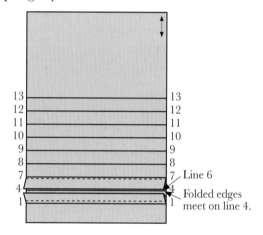

Tip: To keep the work straight and prevent distortion, alternate the sewing direction with each tuck by turning your work. If you sew your first tuck from left to right, sew the next one from right to left. It is not necessary to reapply spray starch or use an iron to press each tuck.

6. Stitch and finger-press the remaining 2 tucks as you did the second one, turning each folded edge down toward the bottom edge of the work.

7. Spray-starch, press, and iron the entire piece.

Mark, Clip, and Point

Use the cutting template on the pullout pattern sheet.

1. Fold the tucked batiste in half lengthwise. Make sure the raw edges are straight and even with each other. Finger-press the fold to mark the center. Unfold.

2. Place the cutting template over the pinning board. Match grain lines and tuck lines, then pin through all layers at each outer corner.

3. Using a newly sharpened pencil with the see-through ruler, mark all 7 perpendicular lines onto the batiste.

4. Draw the basket-handle outline with short broken lines to mark the ribbon placement.

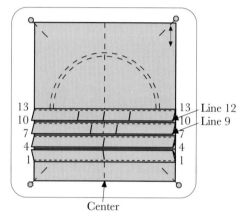

Center

5. Remove the batiste from the pinning board.

6. Beginning on the bottom tuck, cut exactly on the marked line, *stopping 1 thread short of the stitching line.* Fold 1 cut edge under so that the cut edge is parallel to the stitching line and hidden under the tuck. Pin. Finger-press to crease the fold. Repeat with the other cut edge.

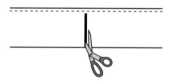

7. Turn the work over and zigzag (SW 1; SL 1) just to one side of the stitching line on the underside of the tuck to catch the cut edges in the stitching. Start stitching 2" (5cm) above the point where you clipped the tuck and end 2" (5cm) below. This stitching outlines the bottom edge of the basket. Be careful not to stitch to the left of the tuck stitching line as you will not catch the raw edges and the tuck will not lie flat on the front of the work.

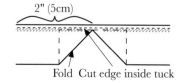

Fold Cut edge inside tuck

8. Repeat steps 6 and 7 on the remaining tucks at the marked cut lines. The illustration below is the finished basket on the right side after cutting, turning, and zigzagging all tucks. An additional row of zigzag stitching can be done over the first zigzagging to secure tucks in place.

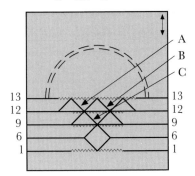

9. Referring to the pattern sheet, zigzag (SW 1.5; SL 0) points A, B, and C in place.

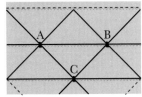

10. Place a ruler alongside the outermost points and mark the basket outline with a sharp pencil. Refer to the pattern as needed. Pin tucks in place and use a straight stitch (SL 2) on the marked line all the way around the basket. To secure the tucks, machine stitch ¼" (6mm) from the outer edges of the batiste. Spray-starch, press, and iron the block.

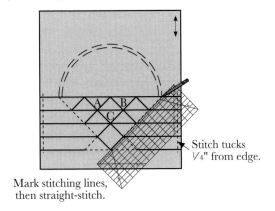

Stitch tucks ¼" from edge.

Mark stitching lines, then straight-stitch.

Couching

1. Lay 6 strands of embroidery floss over the staystitching that defines the outer edges of the basket shape.
2. Zigzag (SW 1.5; SL 1) over the floss and backstitch to secure the ends.

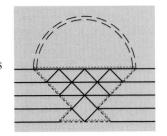

Ribbon Shaping

1. Cut 2 pieces of ribbon, each 4" (10cm) long. Set aside for rosettes, below.
2. Shape and press the ribbon into a basket-handle shape, referring to the directions for ribbon shaping on page 56.

Ribbon Handle

1. Position the shaped ribbon over the handle outline on the batiste, leaving a tail at each end. Pin every ½" (1.25cm.) or so and don't worry if the ribbon does not lie perfectly flat at this point.
2. Trim the ribbon tails to about ¼" (6mm) long, then fold under at line 13 and pin to the batiste.
3. Edgestitch (SL 2) on the outer curved edge of the ribbon.
4. Place the work face down on the towel-covered ironing board and steam-press from the back to ease the excess ribbon into place. Allow to cool.
5. Edgestitch (SL 2) the inside curve of the handle. If necessary, press and iron from the front.
6. Using 3 strands of cotton embroidery floss in your needle, take a small stitch along an edge of the ribbon handle, followed by a long stitch diagonally across the ribbon to the other edge. Repeat to the end of the handle.

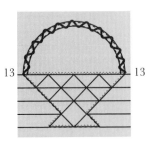

Ribbon Rosettes

Rosettes are easy to make and can be added after the quilting is done.

1. Thread a needle with sewing thread and knot one end. For each rosette, use a 4"-long (10cm) piece of ribbon. Beginning about 1" (5cm) from one end of the ribbon, take a few stitches in place to secure the thread.
2. Do a short running stitch along the ribbon edge, ending 1" (5cm) from the other end. Draw up the stitches to gather into a rosette and bring ends together, taking a few stitches to secure. Fan out the rosette, with ribbon tails extending below, and hand stitch from behind to secure. Use a few hand stitches to sew the rosette to the basket handle. Cut ribbon ends at an angle as shown. Add a cluster of small French knots to the center of each rosette if desired. (See page 65.)

Now that you have completed your beautiful blocks, you are ready to make them into a quilt, adding backing and batting and then quilting by hand or machine. The pencil marks you made as guidelines on each block for construction purposes will still be visible. You will wash the quilt top later to remove these marks. See page 72

Quilt Top Assembly

Materials

3¼ yds. (3m) peach Swiss or Imperial batiste (or other color of your choice, such as pink, blue, yellow, or ecru)

9¼ yds. (8.50m) of ⅝"-wide (1.5cm) lace insertion for sashing between blocks and around outer edges of blocks

6 yds. (5.50m) of 3"-wide (8mm) lace insertion for the floating ribbon lace and bows in the borders

42" x 52" (107cm x 132cm) low-loft cotton or cotton/polyester batting

Assorted buttons, ribbons, and lace edgings for embellishments

#60/2 fine cotton thread

#60/8 universal needle

#100/3 sewing thread

Dixon washout chalk pencil

Straight pins and quilters' safety pins

Pinning board (See page 13.)

Open-toe or clear machine-embroidery foot

Optional: even-feed foot

Template plastic

Scissors and rotary cutter

Permanent marking pen

Ruler and masking tape

Note: Unlike traditional quilts, the Heirloom Quilt is composed of four layers: the top made of twelve batiste sampler blocks, a batiste underlayer, a layer of batting, and a batiste backing. The border of this quilt is actually the batiste layer that lies just beneath the blocks. It extends beyond the outer edges of the blocks and is embellished with floating lace ribbons and bows.

Choose a batting that is compatible with your quilt top. Since Swiss batiste and most of the laces used for heirloom sewing are made of cotton (a natural fiber), the logical choice is a cotton batting. The overall appearance of your quilt will be pleasantly soft and will drape beautifully if you use a 100% cotton batting or an 80% cotton/20% polyester blend.

Look for a batting with the least amount of visible cotton seeds, since they tend to show through the thin layers of fine, sheer fabrics. Check the front of the package for the amount of space to leave unquilted between stitches. The ideal is 2" to 3" (5cm to 7.5cm) between quilted areas. Whatever batting you choose, follow the manufacturer's directions regarding preshrinking.

The batiste backing of this quilt is cut large enough so that you can bind it by folding the extra backing fabric over the edge to the front of the quilt and hand sew it in place.

Preparation

1. Draw a 9¾" x 9¾" (25cm x 25cm) square on template plastic. For accurate cutting and marking, use a rotary ruler and rotary cutter and mat. Using a permanent ink pen, draw diagonal lines from corner to corner on the template. Draw 2 lines through the center of the square, dividing it into 4 equal squares. The halfway point on each side of the square is 4⅞" (12.5cm).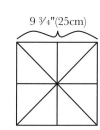

9 ¾"(25cm)

2. Carefully cut out the square. You will use the lines you have drawn to help you position the template over each block for accurate trimming.

3. Center the marked square over a completed block and trace around the outer edges with a fine-point pencil. Repeat with the remaining blocks. *Do not trim yet.*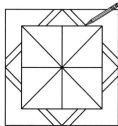

4. Arrange the blocks into 4 rows of 3 blocks each. See the quilt photo on page 37, noting that placement of the individual squares is a personal choice. Your quilt-block layout does not have to match the layout in the quilt plan. Try not to place two blocks side by side that are too similar in design and texture. Alternate the blocks that have more curved lines with those that have straight lines.

Make sure that the lengthwise grain-line markings are all vertical (with the exception of the grain line on the Trellis block, where the grain line will be on the diagonal).

6. When you are pleased with the block layout, remove the Trellis block and staystitch (SL 2) all the way around on the marked line. Replace it in the block layout.

7. Spray-starch, press, and iron the ⅝"-wide (1.5cm) lace insertion for the sashing.

Cutting

From the starched lace insertion, cut:
8 pieces, each 11" (28cm) long, for the vertical sashing between blocks
3 pieces, each 32" (82cm) long, for the horizontal sashing between the rows of blocks.

Sewing

1. Pin an 11"-long (28cm) piece of lace sashing along the drawn lines on the right- and left-hand sides of the center block in each row of blocks. Pin in place. Machine stitch (SL 2) in the lace heading, then zigzag (SW 2; SL .5) over the stitching. Trim away the excess batiste behind the lace close to the zigzagging on the wrong side of the block.

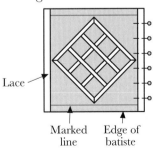

Lace

Marked line   Edge of batiste

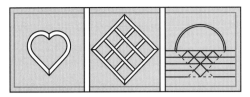

2. Attach the outer blocks in each row to the center block in the same manner (step 1). Press each completed row.

3. Pin and sew the 3 long pieces of lace sashing to the assembled rows of blocks and press.

4. Add lace insertion around the assembled blocks, pinning and mitering the corners as shown in the directions for the Trellis block, beginning on page 30. The quilt top should now measure approximately 31½" x 41½" (80cm x 105cm).

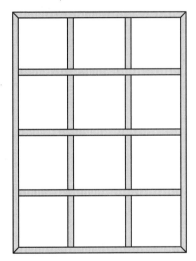

5. Wash the assembled quilt top, following the "General Laundering Directions" in the box on page 72.

6. Press from the back while the fabric is still slightly damp, using spray starch if necessary. Check the back of the quilt top and trim away any remaining batiste behind the lace.

7. Prewash the 3¼ yards (3m) of batiste and lace for the bow in a tub. See "General Laundering Directions" on page 72. Iron and set aside. Preshrink the batting, following the manufacturer's directions.

General Laundering Directions

The old-fashioned way of laundering cotton heirloom garments was to use boiling water and white soap. It is no wonder that some of these antique clothes look like they went through a war zone. Today, we have so many new detergents to make washing easier and gentler on the garment. Hand wash fabric and trimmings with a mild liquid detergent like Ivory, Delicare, LeBlanc Linen Wash, Easy Wash, or Orvus, following the manufacturer's directions.

1. In a clean bathtub, draw lukewarm water and dissolve the detergent.
2. Place the loosely folded quilt top in the soapy water, unfold, and gently swish. Allow to soak until the markings disappear, leaving in the water overnight if necessary. The light coating of starch on the blocks makes it easier to remove the dots and lines you drew on each block for positioning purposes. For stubborn stains, you can add a drop of detergent or make a paste of baking soda and water to rub lightly on the stained area.
3. Drain the soapy water, isolating the quilt top from the flow of water. Refill the tub with cool water in order to rinse out any soapy residues. Swish fabric gently but do not wring or lift out of the water. At this point, the water has weakened the fibers and weighs heavily on the batiste and laces.
4. Drain the rinse water. Support the fabric to relieve stress and transfer to a towel. Lay a second towel on top if necessary, to absorb excess water. Roll all layers together, unroll, and place over a clean white sheet. Let dry until damp, then press.

If laundering smaller items, such as a single quilt block, a handkerchief, or lace strips, use a kitchen colander. Place the item to be laundered in the colander; immerse into the soapy water. Let soak and rinse as described in steps 2–4. The colander allows the water to seep through and drain easily while supporting the wet fabric.

Note: If you need to launder the completed quilt after it has been used or stored with mothballs, sandwich it between two layers of cheesecloth and hand baste the layers together. This alleviates the stress created by the weight when wet and the motion required for hand washing.

8. Following the cutting diagram, cut the pieces for the quilt top underlayer, backing, and hanging sleeves (if you wish to make this into a wall hanging).

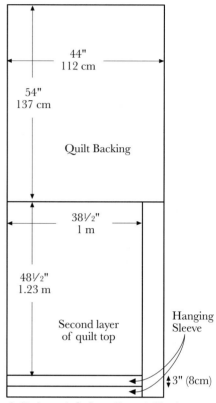

3¼ yds (3m) peach Swiss or Imperial batiste

9. Use small pieces of masking tape to attach the quilt-top underlayer to a hard surface. You want to keep it taut, but do not overstretch. Center the assembled blocks on top. Pin the layers together, working from the center out and smoothing the layers to remove any wrinkles. Remove the tape.
10. Staystitch (SL 2.5) in the outer lace heading of the mitered lace insertion all the way around the quilt top. Zigzag (SW 2; SL 1) over the straight stitching. You may also use the mending/serpentine stitch (SW 5 and SL 1) inside the lace sashing as shown at the top of page 73. Begin with the inner sashing, then do the outer pieces.

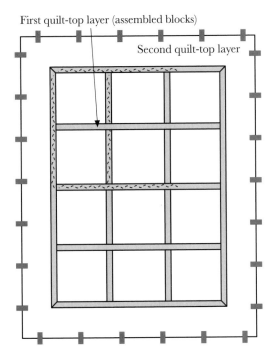

First quilt-top layer (assembled blocks)

Second quilt-top layer

Bow Shaping

Use the pattern on page 75.

1. Place the bow pattern on the pinning board and carefully slip the board under one corner of the quilt top. Do not trace the bow design onto the batiste, as you have already laundered the quilt top. Anchor the fabric to the pattern and pinning board with pins.

2. Using one continuous piece of lace insertion and following the bow-shaping directions for the Bow block on page 17, shape a bow. Continue shaping the tails by folding the lace back at the angle on the pattern, ½" (1.25cm) from the lace insertion at the outer edge of the blocks and 2" (5cm) away from the vertical and horizontal lace sashing strips as shown in the diagram below. Be careful not to stretch the lace as you pin.

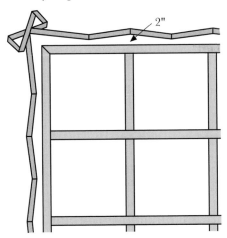

2"

3. Continue shaping and pinning the bows and floating lace tail all the way around until you reach the first corner. Move the pinning board and pattern as needed. Slip the tail under the center of the bow and trim excess. Pin.

4. Use a straight stitch (SL 2) in the lace headings. Do not cut away the batiste behind this lace insertion as the batting will be exposed. Press. This is your last chance to remove any creases or wrinkles from the quilt top before adding the batting.

5. Optional: You may add a lace rosette to the center of each bow. See page 18 for directions.

Layering

1. Tape the backing to a flat surface. Do not trim away the selvage edges on the backing sections. If needed, clip into the selvage edge if it is taut and will not lie flat.

2. Lay the batting on top of the backing. *Center the quilt top over the two layers.* Working from the center out, smooth away any unwanted puckers and wrinkles. Pin or hand baste the layers together, working from the center out.

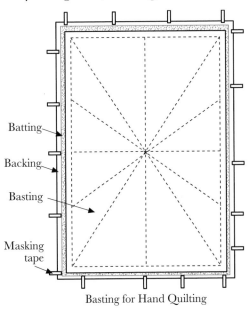

Batting

Backing

Basting

Masking tape

Basting for Hand Quilting

QUILTING

Quilting is the process of stitching the quilt top, batting, and backing together. Besides holding all these layers together, it adds beauty and dimension to the quilt.

Basic quilting information is included here for hand and machine quilting. For more information on hand quilting, see *Loving Stitches* by Jeana Kimball.

For the purist, hand quilting is the only choice. This quilt is small enough for lap quilting and with the use of a small hoop, you can quilt just about anywhere. Hand quilting can have a very therapeutic and soothing effect on one's soul. The hand stitching and slow pace are reminiscent of a gentler, unhurried era. Master hand quilting by taking some classes at your local quilt shop or quilting guild and by practicing.

If time is a factor, machine quilting can be the answer. (Perhaps the baby is already on the way and you don't have time to hand quilt this special gift.) Machine quilting takes a fraction of the time required for hand quilting. Machine quilting is not new. It has been around for over one hundred years and was executed on large machines.

To showcase the heirloom laces and designs, use shadow, echo, and in-the-ditch quilting, whether you stitch by hand or machine.

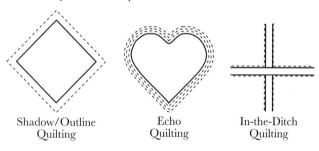

Shadow/Outline Quilting   Echo Quilting   In-the-Ditch Quilting

Before you do any quilting in the blocks, stitch in-the-ditch on each side of the lace sashing. To avoid puckering, work from the center out toward the edge as much as possible.

Refer to the block photos on pages 38–40 or plan your own quilting patterns for each block.

BINDING

1. Staystitch ¼" (6mm) from the outer edges of the quilt top and batting through all layers. Trim away the excess batting. Trim the backing so that it extends 2½" from the quilt top edge all around.

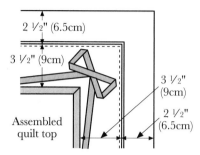

2 ½" (6.5cm)
3 ½" (9cm)
3 ½" (9cm)
2 ½" (6.5cm)
Assembled quilt top

2. Remove all the basting stitches or pins.
3. To begin the self-binding process, fold each corner at a 45° angle so that the backing corner point meets the corner of the quilt. Finger-press to crease; cut on the fold.

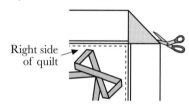

Right side of quilt

4. Fold the trimmed corner to meet the stitching line at the corner.

5. Bring the adjacent edges of the backing to the front to meet the trimmed edge of the quilt top.

6. Fold again so that the upper folded edge just covers the stitching line. Repeat the procedure for the adjoining edge. A miter will form at the corner. Pin the binding in place. Slipstitch the self binding in place all the way around the quilt.

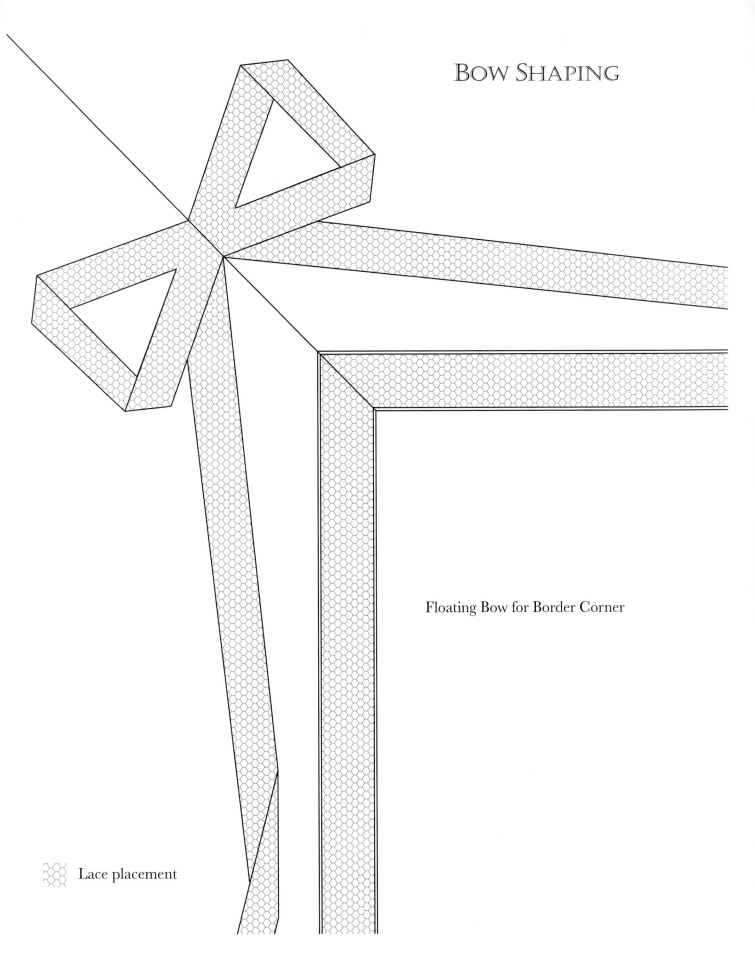

Floating Bow for Border Corner

Lace placement

Hanging Sleeve

1. Turn under and press ¼" (6mm) at each end of each of the two 3"-wide strips of batiste. Turn and press again and stitch close to the inner fold.

2. Fold the tube in half lengthwise with wrong sides together and raw edges even. Stitch ¼" (6mm) from the raw edges. Press the seam open, then press the tube so the seam is centered on the wrong side.

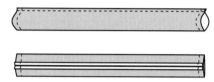

3. Slipstitch one tube to the back of the quilt at the top edge and the other to the bottom edge.

4. Slip a dowel or slat inside the top sleeve for hanging and into the bottom sleeve to add weight.

Labeling Your Quilt
A Stitch in Time

It is important to add a label to the back of the quilt identifying the maker, the date completed, the name of the recipient, and any other pertinent information. Type, write, or embroider this information on a scrap of laundered and pressed fabric and slipstitch it to the back of the quilt. Make the fabric piece large enough so that future generations can register additional information as this precious heirloom is passed on. This family history is sure to be appreciated for generations to come.

Another special way to keep this information safe is by making a Handkerchief Keepsake Envelope to sew to the back of the completed quilt.

Handkerchief Keepsake Envelope

Store baby's birth announcement and baptism certificate along with special pictures of the happy event in this pretty fabric envelope. Consider embroidering the baby's name and birth date on the envelope flap. Add special photographs and other mementos to the envelope as you wish. Be sure to wrap all items in acid-free tissue before tucking them inside the envelope.

Materials

1 embroidered handkerchief (any size) with a finished rolled edge (no lace edges, please)
#100/3 sewing thread
½ yd. (46cm) narrow ribbon
Open-toe or clear machine-embroidery foot
1 button* or a lace or satin rosette for a closure
#60/8 sewing-machine needle
#60/2 fine embroidery thread for recording the baby's name and date of birth on the envelope flap

OR

Permanent marking pen to record this information

*Select a relatively flat button if you are hanging the quilt on the wall.

Directions

1. With right sides together, fold the hanky in half, with the edge of the bottom layer extending ⅛" (3mm) beyond the edge of the top layer, at the end without the embroidered design.

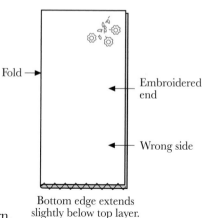

Fold →

Embroidered end →

Wrong side →

Bottom edge extends slightly below top layer.

Using the #100/3 sewing thread, zigzag (SW 3; SL 1) over the rolled edges on one side only.

2. Open the hanky and refold to form a triangle shape at one end. Then fold one corner (the one without the embroidery) to meet the center seam. Pin the two rolled edges together and zigzag as shown in step 1. You should have an envelope shape when completed. Turn right side out.

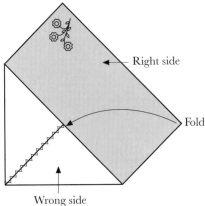

Right side

Fold

Wrong side

3. Press carefully to avoid stretching the hanky. Fold in half lengthwise to find the true center and finger-press to crease.

4. Bring the embroidered corner down to meet the bottom of the envelope at the center. Press.

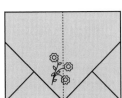

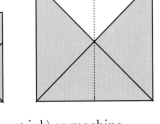

5. Write (with permanent ink) or machine embroider on the flap any information that you wish to add at this point. Change to #60/2 thread if embroidering, or slip a piece of paper under the area where you will write to prevent ink from seeping through to the envelope.

6. Make a knot at each end of the ribbon and fold in half to find the center. Finger-press.

7. At the flap point, turn under ¼" (6mm) and bar-tack the center of the ribbon to both layers of the hanky. Sew a button (or a lace or satin rose) to the bottom edge of the envelope. Tie the ribbon around the button in a bow.

8. Hand sew the completed envelope to the backing of your quilt.

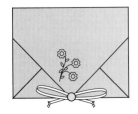

During the Victorian era, it was customary to wear a lock of hair from a loved one. If you wish to continue this tradition, tie a lock of the loved one's hair with a bow, add a label with the person's name, wrap in acid-free tissue, and tuck into the Handkerchief Keepsake Envelope.

CARING FOR YOUR QUILT

If you plan to hang the quilt on the wall, locate it away from direct sunlight and high-traffic areas. To prolong its life, take the quilt outside from time to time for some fresh air.

If you wish to store the quilt for any period of time, do the following:

1. Ask your local fabric store for an empty cardboard fabric tube or check with a carpet store for an empty carpet tube.

2. Wrap the tube in laundered, unbleached muslin or cotton fabric.

3. Place a clean white cotton sheet or a large piece of laundered, unbleached muslin on a flat surface.

4. Place acid-free tissue paper on top of the cotton sheet. Then place your quilt right side down on the paper and roll loosely over the muslin covered tubing.

5. Store the extra fabric at the ends along with a small bar of soap (from your latest hotel stay) inside the tube at each end. The higher the perfume content in the soap, the more repugnant your quilt will be to unwanted insects!

6. Store the rolled quilt in a cool, dry place with adequate ventilation.

Caution: Do not store precious heirlooms in plastic. It does not breathe like cotton.

~ HEIRLOOM PROJECTS ~

Although the blocks in this book were designed specifically for a quilt, you can use the designs for many other creative projects, limited only by your imagination.

PROJECT IDEAS

Described below are several project ideas. You can probably think of many other ways to use the blocks. Color photos of several of them appear on pages 41–44.

Table Runner

Join three to five blocks with lace sashing to form one long strip. Add lace edging to the outer edges.

Pillow

Add strips of fabric to the outer edges of one finished block to make it pillow size. As pictured on page 42, the envelope-style pillow is very Victorian and a pretty alternative.

Square Tablecloth

Sew four or nine blocks together with lace sashing as described for the quilt top to make a tablecloth of the desired size.

Curtains

Insert one or more blocks in the border of batiste curtain panels or in a valance.

Lampshade Cover

Add lace edging around one block and place over a small lampshade. This is a very French, boudoir look.

Purse, Lingerie Bag, or Evening Bag

Make any of these items from a single square, referring to the "Handkerchief Keepsake Envelope" directions on page 76.

Tea Cozy

Use some of the heirloom techniques in this book to create a lace design on quilted fabric pieces cut for a tea cozy. See *Tea Party Time* by Nancy J. Martin for tea-cozy directions.

Duvet Cover

To eliminate the necessity of quilting the finished project, make a duvet cover from the twelve blocks for a baby-size comforter.

Handkerchief

Use one of the block designs to make a handkerchief for a special bride. Later, the hanky can be made into a baby bonnet for the first-born child.

TIC-TAC-TOE BOARD GAME

This is a wonderful game for little girls' tea parties. It stores flat and is washable! Hand-painted flower buttons are used as playing pieces for the game shown in the photo on page 44.

Materials

1 piece of Swiss batiste, 9" (23cm) square
1⅝ yds. (152cm) of ½"-wide (1.25cm) lace insertion
⅞ yd. (80cm) of ¾"-wide (2cm) lace edging
10 buttons, beads, or seashells (5 each of 2 different colors) for playing pieces
Appliqué scissors
#60/8 sewing-machine needles
#60/2 cotton embroidery thread
Dixon washout chalk pencil
Fine silk pins
Pinning Board (See page 13).
Ruler
Open-toe or clear machine-embroidery foot

Directions

1. Follow the directions for making the trellis in the Trellis block, beginning on page 29.
2. When finished, butt lace edging to the outside edge of the square, mitering the corners as described for the block, and zigzag (SW 2; SL .5).
3. Trim away any excess batiste that shows behind the lace edging.

Note: Roll the completed board game over a paper tube with the playing pieces tucked inside the tubing in a reclosable plastic bag when not in use. If you wish to store the whole game in a larger plastic bag, remember to leave an opening to allow the fabric to breathe.

If your local sewing center does not carry the fabrics, trimmings, and sewing notions required for this quilt, write to the following sources for a mail-order catalog or call for ordering information.

RETAIL AND MAIL-ORDER SOURCES

General Sewing Supplies & Tools

Clotilde
1909 S.W. 1st Avenue
Fort Lauderdale, FL 33315-2100
USA

Nancy's Notions
333 Beichel Avenue
PO Box 683
Beaver Dam, WI 53916-0683
USA
1-800-833-0690

Laces & Heirloom Fabrics

Lacis
2982 Adeline Street, Dept. JM
Berkeley, CA 99703
USA

Martha Pullen Company, Inc.
518 Madison Street
Huntsville, AL 35801
USA

Wholesale Only
Capitol Imports, Tallahassee, FL
1-800-521-7647

All fabrics and trimmings used in the Heirloom Sampler Quilt are from Capitol Imports. Please call the 800 number for information concerning the nearest dealer that carries Capitol products.

Custom Heirloom Sewing
Keepsake Treasures
c/o Karen Janis
22945 Lochanora Drive
Hawthorn Woods, IL 60047

Cairns, Pat. *Contemporary Quilting Techniques.* Radnor, Pa.: Chilton Book Company, 1991.

Duke, Dennis, and Deborah Harding. *America's Glorious Quilts* New York: Park Lane/Crown Publishers, Inc., 1989.

Fanning, Robbie and Tony. *The Complete Book of Machine Quilting.* Radnor, Pa.: Chilton Book Company, 1980.

Foley, Tricia. *Linen and Lace.* New York City, New York: Clarkson N. Pottor Inc., 1990.

Hart, Cynthia, and Catherine Calvert. *The Love of Lace.* New York: Workman Publishing, 1992.

Hart, Cynthia, John Grossman, and Priscilla Dunhill. *A Victorian Scrapbook.* New York: Workman Publishing Co., 1989.

Kratz, Anne. *Lace,* originally published in France as *Dentelles.* New York: Rizzoli International Publications, Inc., 1989.

Martin, Nancy J. *Tea Party Time.* Bothell, Wash.: That Patchwork Place, 1992.

Montano, Judith. *The Crazy Quilt Handbook.* Lafayette, Co.: C and T Publishing, 1986.

Parker, Freda. *Victorian Embroidery.* New York: Crescent Books, 1991.

Parker, Freda. *Victorian Patchwork.* London: Anaya Publishers Ltd., 1991.

That Patchwork Place Publications and Products

Many titles are available at your local quilt shop. For more information, send $2 for a color catalog to That Patchwork Place, Inc., PO Box 118, Bothell WA 98041-0118 USA.

☎ Call 1-800-426-3126 for the name and location of the quilt shop nearest you.